British
Battle Cruisers

Peter C. Smith

ALMARK PUBLISHING CO. LTD., LONDON

First published—October 1972

By the same author:

Stuka at War

Task Force 57

Destroyer Leader

Pedestal

Hard Lying

ISBN 0 85524 082 2 (hard cover edition)

ISBN 0 85524 083 0 (paper covered edition)

Author's dedication:
For
Dawn Tracey

Printed in Great Britain by
The Byron Press Ltd., 59 Palmerston Road, Wealdstone, Middx.
for the publishers, Almark Publishing Co. Ltd.,
270 Burlington Road, New Malden, Surrey KT3 4N4, England

Foreword

BATTLE CRUISER. The name conjures up many pictures in one's mind. Sleek, enormous warships steaming at full speed through the tumbling water of the grey North Sea. A quiet, powerful vessel, brasswork gleaming, slipping out of Gibraltar Bay. The split-second annihilation of a thousand men in a searing explosion of fire and flame. The Battle Cruiser story is all these and more.

Their life-span was among the briefest of any warship type but in a forty-year period they graced the world's oceans and captured the imagination of seaman and landsman alike.

To obtain the true flavour of life aboard the Battle Cruiser in all its many facets one should read *With the Battle Cruisers* by Filson Young or *The Mighty Hood* By Ernle Bradford. This little book cannot convey that flavour but is an attempt to record in one compact volume, the background story of the British Battle Cruiser while the selection of photographs will, it is hoped, provide a lasting record of the grandeur and majesty of these great vessels.

Author and publisher wish to thank John Dominy for the scale drawings, Tom Stone and Arthur North for the colour art, and the Imperial War Museum photo-library, and Mr. E. C. Hine for assistance in selecting the photographs. Catalogue numbers (where known) of Imperial War Museum (IWM) pictures are given and 6″ x 4″ size prints may be ordered from the museum at 20p each.

CONTENTS

Section	Page
Foreword	
1: Fisher	5
2: The *Invincible* Class	8
3: The *Indefatigable* Class	15
4: The *Lion* Class	24
5: The *Tiger*	30
6: Beatty	32
7: The *Renown* Class	36
8: The *Courageous* Class	42
9: The Battle Cruiser at War	46
10: The *Hood*	64
11: The *1921* Battle Cruisers	67
12: *Renown* and *Repulse* Modified	68
13: The Passing of the Giants	71
Appendix One: Comparison Table.	80
Appendix Two: The German Ships.	80
Appendix Three: Battle Cruiser Pendants.	80

ABOVE: The sleek lines of HMS Repulse, *in a dockyard basin at Portsmouth, in 1934, are well emphasised in this view which also shows her two 15 inch forward turrets, conning tower, and triple 4 inch high angle turrets. FRONT COVER: Another view of this ship in 1937 when she carried red/white/blue neutrality stripes on 'B' turret, used to distinguish British ships near Spanish waters in the Civil War period. BACK COVER:* Invincible *and* Inflexible *during the chase of Von Spee's squadron, December 8, 1914 (IWM-Q45912).*

1: Fisher

ALTHOUGH the life-span of the Battle Cruiser as a distinct type of warship was only of a brief duration, only ten years actually separating the laying down of the first and the last of these vessels for the Royal Navy, these great ships caught the imagination of the public in a way that few others have done before or since.

The battle cruisers merited this attention for they were indeed remarkable products of man's skill combining speed and beauty with an impression of enormous power. That they had inbuilt weaknesses was not at first generally apparent. The few doubting voices went unheeded in this the period of the naval arms race which preceded World War I, the Battle Cruisers' ultimate proving ground.

To a major extent these ships were the products and creations of that tempestuous genius Admiral Sir John Fisher. 'Jackie' Fisher had been appointed to the post of First Sea Lord on Trafalgar Day 1904 and he arrived at the Admiralty determined to put into effect all the many ideas and reforms which he had been advocating for so many years. The man radiated energy and had complete faith in his mission, which he saw as the bringing of the Royal Navy to a perfect pitch in readiness for the inevitable struggle with the arrogant Kaiser Wilhelm's Germany.

He advocated many reforms which he determined would drag the Navy into the twentieth century and he possessed the single-mindedness and strength of character to carry through most of them despite considerable opposition.

Among his ideas which bore fruit were the building of the Royal Naval Colleges at Osborn and Dartmouth and the introduction of corresponding systems of education. He persisted in the wise course of concentrating the main fighting strength of the Royal Navy in Home Waters on the eve of the Great War and he was also ruthless in the advocacy of cutting away the 'dead wood' which encumbered the Fleet with ships too old to serve as anything other than targets for the enemy.

But on assuming the mantle of First Sea Lord his most startling changes of policy became manifest in his proposed construction programmes for the new navy he deemed necessary. Fisher was obsessed with the value of the combination of speed and firepower, which in itself was very laudable. Unfortunately in warship construction for every plus there must be a balancing minus and in Fisher's concept of things that minus was protection.

He had already applied himself to the attaining of greater accuracy in ships' gunnery with good results but he was to become over-enthusiastic with his pursuit of speed. The walls of Fisher's office were hung with placards which reflected his offensive spirit, and one such slogan, above all, gave the key to the emergence of the Battle Cruisers:

'Hit first; Hit hard; and keep on Hitting!'

Lord Nelson was one of Fisher's idols and the complete annihilation of the enemy was his ultimate aim in warfare. Fisher was convinced that in the struggle to come with the upstart young Navy of Imperial Germany the ability

The 1st Battle Cruiser Squadron at sea, in line ahead, 1914

to get in the first blow accurately would decide the issue. At the same time the British Fleet must always be able to decide and dictate the range of position of the combat and for this speed was the key.

It must be held in mind that the Royal Navy at this period was only just settling down after emerging from almost thirty years of turmoil and change during which the grip of technology had fastened overpoweringly on naval design. Gone were the tried and tested 'Wooden Walls and Broadsides' on which Britain's unassailable position as the world's premier naval power had been based. It had only been in 1895 that a stable battleship design had emerged from the welter of half-formed ideas and experiments, these were Sir William White's magnificent 'Majestic' class ships which had set the pattern for ten years.

It can therefore be readily understood that the sudden appearance of Fisher's famous *Dreadnought* caused a furore throughout naval circles both at home and abroad. This battleship at one stroke rendered obsolete all the 4 x 12 inch, 12 x 6 inch, 17-knot battleships which Britain had laboriously built up over the years and of which she possessed in 1906, a decisive margin over her rivals.

Fisher and the Admiralty Board were bitterly criticised for largely outmoding Britain's existing naval strength, but in truth such a large vessel had long been discussed in naval circles and indeed the United States was already proceeding with a similar sort of design when *Dreadnought* was announced. By coming out first with the new ship, developed in secrecy, Fisher had hoped to ensure a vital lead in construction which Britain could exploit before her rivals, but especially Germany, could reorganise their existing building programmes. Alas, as so often happens, political vacillation threw this trump away.

But it was not solely in battleship design that Fisher's new concepts were applied but right across the whole range of naval design and philosophy. The old idea of 'close blockade' was not finally abandoned until the eve of World War I. However, it was already outmoded by vast increases in the range of naval guns combined with improved accuracy and standards which had been worked out by keen gunnery officers like Admiral Sir Percy Scott, a protegé of Fisher. A distant blockade was envisaged by Fisher and existing types like the small 'protected' cruisers were to be done away with and large destroyers types, like the *Swift* and the 'Tribals', were to take their place. The increased use of W/T would bridge the gaps in such a blockade and should the enemy break free distant covering forces would be directed to complete his destruction.

Two years prior to his appointment as First Sea Lord Fisher had already put forward the basis of a new type intended to replace the traditional 'armoured' cruiser types already in service. These large costly ships had grown progressively until they had reached the status of Second-Class Battleships, the last of them mounting a combination of 9·2 inch and 7·5 inch guns on a 14,000 tons displacement at 23 knots top speed.

The origin of the armoured cruiser had originally been to combat fast French commerce raiders on Britain's distant trade routes but the arguments which led to the replacement of the existing battleships by *Dreadnought* applied equally well to the armoured cruiser. Again it was known that new designs were contemplated abroad and it was learnt that the Japanese were building vessels of this nature designed to mount 4 x 12 inch and 12 x 6 inch guns at 21 knots.

It can thus be seen that had Britain not proceeded with the first 'Improved Armoured Cruisers', as they were initially known, the country would have been faced, as with the American 'Michigans' in battleship design, with a foreign *coup*. Thanks to Fisher it was the Royal Navy which astonished the world with the completion of the *Invincible*.

Although the basic tasks of hunting commerce raiders still held good as a primary task for the first battle cruisers it was the rise of the German High Seas Fleet which led to the role of these vessels in the Royal Navy to be enlarged to encompass their use as the fast wings of the battle fleet. In this new role the battle cruisers were to force their way up to within sight of the enemy fleet using their superior firepower to brush aside the enemy cruiser screen and to report back the enemy fleet's composition and other relevant data to the C-in-C.

It was also felt that the battle cruiser would act as support for smaller scouting cruisers and also act themselves as fast shadowing vessels following a fleeing enemy fleet and ensuring the destruction of damaged enemy ships. Fisher never envisaged an enemy fleet being anything other than 'fleeing' from a British one and the British public would never dream of anything else. So the fact that these tasks relied on the ability of the new type to keep out of range of the main enemy fleet was overlooked. To do this and to outgun all likely defending vessels meant heavy guns and excessive speed but only limited *protection* as they were only to operate on the fringes of the enemy battle fleet—in theory!

Into this argument Fisher cast the decision that an all big-gun version of his new *Dreadnought* design, given a speed of 25 knots would ensure the immunity of the new vessels as nothing which could sink them could catch them. Consideration was given to no less than five different designs, the best of which would result in the final realisation of Fishers 'ideal' which he named HMS *Uncatchable*.

2: The 'Invincible' Class

TO prepare the new type along Fisher's lines a Committee of Design was called upon to consider the five alternatives all of which presented the desired dispositon of armament. The requirement called for not less than four guns to command the forward or after arcs with four to six abeam. The Fisher design worked out with the Chief Constructor, W. H. Gard, showed a novel turret layout with the twin 12 inch guns in paired turrets forward, with twin mountings *super-firing* aft. This layout showed vision for which the Board was not yet ready and was rejected on grounds of blast interference.

The construction department put forward three alternate designs which also featured twin turrets mounted abreast. In design 'B' eight 12 inch guns were mounted thus, grouped fore and aft, while in design 'C', which was a cut-down version, one after turret was dropped and the paired twin mountings forward were brought back to increase seaworthiness. Similar arrangements had been tried out in other nations' vessels and the whole idea was considered objectionable.

Design 'D' produced eight 12 inch guns in twin turrets situated forward, aft and two midships turrets which were placed abreast. This layout, in the light of opposition to super-firing positions, gave the best broadside fire and was adopted with modifications as design 'E' which placed the midships turrets diagonally. This provided the best all-round fire at the expense of a strong broadside.

The final basis on which the first battle cruisers were laid down called for the addition of a long foc's'le which was extended well aft giving the midships guns a better command and the ships themselves improved seaworthiness. The striking clipper bow shown in all these designs was replaced with a ram for appearance sake as in the *Dreadnought,* a retrograde step which was not finally dropped until the *Hood,* but which enhanced the impression of latent power.

Inflexible, Indomitable.   *IWM–SP2880.*   *1918*

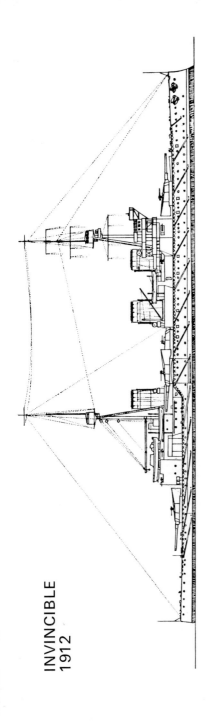

INVINCIBLE
1912

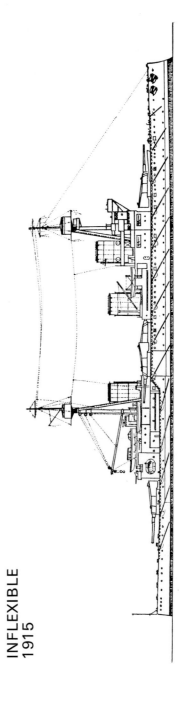

INFLEXIBLE
1915

Thus the 1905 programme called for the building of three of these ships, as revolutionary in their way as was the *Dreadnought* herself, although they were still officially referred to as 'Armoured Cruisers'. No details were forthcoming during their construction but the impression got about that they would mount a much improved armament based on the well-tried 9·2 inch gun. As a reply to this the German *Blücher* was laid down mounting twelve 8·2 inch guns.

When the *Invincible* was finally unveiled there was still considerable opposition to her and some uncertainty as to just what role these enormous and expensive vessels were to play in modern war. Indeed even at the outbreak of war some six years later Admiral Beatty was still conducting exercises and seeking a satisfactory role for his new command.

The *Invincible's* protection was on 'armoured cruiser' scale and amounted to an amidships belt six inches deep reducing to four inches at the extremities with a three inch armoured deck. The turrets had 7 inch protection and the decks only a maximum of $2\frac{1}{2}$ inches.

This was of course to be the ships undoing although it was adequate for the somewhat nebulous role for which they had been designed. It was soon feared however that such huge costly ships would almost certainly find themselves in the front rank of future battles and here their speed would be negated and their protection completely useless.

Such shortcomings—which later led to tragic losses—were much commented upon at the time and the potential weakness of this type of vessel was common knowledge throughout the British fleet long before Jutland.

To give a theoretical four knot margin of speed over the *Dreadnought* required an increase in length of 34 feet, 18,000 more horse-power and the elimination of one 12 inch turret as well as the armour sacrifice. In fact all these ships exceeded their design speeds by a healthy margin and this was to reap dividends at the Falkland Islands battle although Filson Young was later to record in *With the Battle Cruisers*:

'We never really caught up with the German battle cruisers when they were running away from us at full speed. It takes a long time, and a huge distance has to be covered, if a ship going at high speed is to be overtaken by a slightly faster one of which she has the start. In the case of a ship steaming at 24 knots, having a twenty mile start of a ship steaming at 26 knots, it would take just five hours, and 130 knots would have to be covered in a stern chase, before the twenty miles were reduced to ten—the beginning of effective gunnery range'.

The average cost of these ships was £1,640,000 and in fact they fulfilled their design well and were copied all too quickly by the Germans, who however, placed greater emphasis on their fast Battle Fleet Wing role than did the British with their wider horizons.

OPPOSITE: A fine view of the forward turret, conning tower, and bridge, of Inflexible *in 1915. In the foreground is one of the cable holders used to let go and recover the anchor. The slots in the top of the spindle took a lever for clutching and de-clutching the cable holder from the drive spindle — the holder was de-clutched to let the anchor and cable run out under its own weight. The 12 inch guns are sealed by their tompions which have an embossed ship's crest. Note the 4 inch guns on the turret top. The sighting ports for the gun and turret layer's periscopes can be clearly seen. On the bridge wings are semaphore signal posts.*

As with all British battle cruisers these ships were generally held to have much greater protection than really existed, the *Invincible* commonly being credited with 7 inch belts and 10 inch turrets. While this may have taken in uninformed observers, expert opinion was hostile.

In 1912 Sir William White wrote of these ships;

> 'Opinions differed and still differ in regard to the policy of building such large and costly cruisers, (The term 'Battle Cruiser' had not yet been generally adopted), and of endowing them with very high speed, if they are primarily intended to take part in Fleet actions'.[1]

To show that this was a widely held viewpoint, *Brassey's Naval Annual* made the same telling point;

> 'Vessels of this enormous size and cost are unsuited for many of the duties of cruisers, but an even stronger objection to the repetition of the type is that an admiral having 'Invincibles' in his fleet will be certain to put them in the line of battle, where their comparatively light protection would be a disadvantage and their high speed of no value'.[*]

Admiral Schofield, writing more recently, roundly condemns them as '. . . a blunder'. He states that when he joined the *Indomitable* in 1912 the weakness of the design was a matter of common knowledge among the officers.[2] Winston Churchill has recorded that he, 'recoiled from the Battle Cruiser type,' although that did not later prevent him refering to them as the 'Strategic cavalry of the Royal Navy'.[3]

The official viewpoint was put by Admiral Sir Henry Jackson who was then Third Sea Lord and Controller. In a paper to the Board he laid down that;

> 'The *Invincible* class must be regarded as fast battleships rather than armoured cruisers'.[4]

Indeed this was the attitude of both the public and many seamen at the time. In fairness Oscar Parkes was to record:

> 'Fisher's "Speed is the best protection" would have kept the ships at maximum range, but when the occasion arose for gallant leadership in the face of the enemy the dictates of design were brushed aside and the *Invincible* steamed at full speed into annihilation'.[5]

Ship	Builder	Laid Down	Launched	Completed
Indomitable	Fairfield	1.3.06	16.3.07	25.6.08
Inflexible	Clydebank	5.2.06	26.6.07	20.10.08
Invincible	Elswick	2.4.06	13.4.07	20.3.08

Dimensions: 530′ (567′ OA) x 78′ 6″ x 25′ 6″ / 26′ 9″.
Displacement: 17,250 tons (Navy List).
Armament: 8 x 12 inch/45; 16 x 4 inch/45; 1 x 3 inch; 5 x 18 inch TT.
Machinery: Parsons turbines, 41,000 hp = 25 knots.
Complement: 784.

[1]*Brassey's Naval Annual* (1912,) [2]*British Sea Power* (Batsford, 1967). [3]*The World Crisis* (Cassel, 1923). [4]*The Fisher Papers. Vol. 2* (Naval Records Society). [5]*British Battleships* (Oscar Parkes, Seeley Service, 1957).

INDOMITABLE
1918

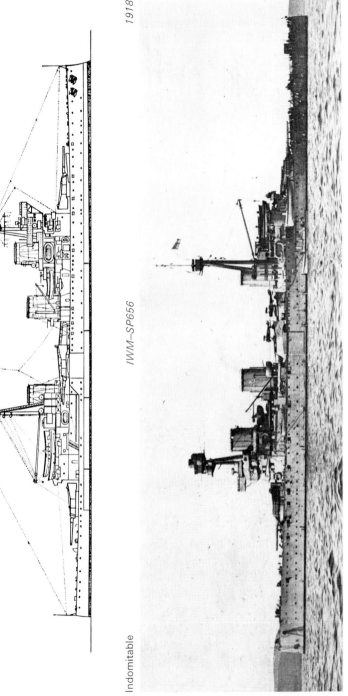

1918

IWM–SP656

Indomitable

13

Inflexible (coaling ship at Mudros)   1915   IWM—Q13815

Inflexible   1912   IWM—Q39240

14

3:The 'Indefatigable' Class

DUE to the experience gained in the construction of the 'Invincibles' these three ships worked out cheaper to build, averaging £1,343,000 apiece but this was the sole advantage gained. A great deal of controversy had taken place over the 1908 building programme and as a result the *Australia* and *New Zealand* were subscribed for by their respective countries, the latter being formally handed over to the Royal Navy while the former served as flagship of the Australian Navy although she was allocated to the Grand Fleet for the major part of her war service.

Reputed while building to be 'wonder ships' with improved armour, in-

Indefatigable   *IWM–Q39269*   *1912*

ABOVE AND OPPOSITE: Coaling ship in Australia. *'Coal Ship' was a major evolution in the early years of the 'steam' Navy before oil-firing became common. All hands were normally employed on this evolution and there was considerable competition among ships of the same squadron to be first to complete. Old clothing was worn, often non-regulation style. Ships of this class took over 3,000 tons of coal into their bunkers at a full loading, a massive non-stop operation. The coal was tipped into the bunkers through manholes in the deck (IWM-Q18754 and Q18753).*

creased armament and speed and 'motor driven' they were in the words of Oscar Parkes;

    ' . . . nothing but an enlarged *Invincible* with the same weak protection and presenting a larger target'.*

The two wing turrets were placed further apart which in theory gave a wider arc of fire on the beam, while the secondary armament was installed in the fore and after superstructures. With a 6 inch belt, 7 inch turrets and 2 inch decks her coal bunkerage was around 3,000 tons and speeds of up to 29 knots were reached. The last two vessels were completed late when their usefulness was already in doubt. Fisher's dictum:

    'Build few and build fast, each one better than the last', can therefore be seen to have fallen down with the *Indefatigable's*. All very fine for him to write with tremendous enthusiasm;

British Battleships (op cit).

'I've got Sir Philip Watts into a new *Indomitable* that will make your mouth water when you see it, and the Germans gnash their teeth'.[1]

The German reaction was the *Von der Tann* with a $9\frac{3}{4}$ inch belt and $3\frac{3}{4}$ inch deck armour while only a knot slower.

The 'Indefatigables' were aggressive-looking ships and good sea boats but if anything their construction was a greater folly than the 'Invincibles' whose design was already approaching obsolescence with the construction of the first German Battle Cruisers.

Ship	Builder	Laid Down	Launched	Completed
Indefatigable	Devonport	23.2.09	28.10.09	2.11
Australia	John Brown	23.6.10	25.10.11	6.13
New Zealand	Fairfield	20.6.10	1.7.11	11.12

Dimensions:	555′ (590′ OA) x 80′ x 24·75′ (27′).
Displacement:	18,800 tons (designed).
Armament:	8 x 12 inch/50; 16 x 4 inch/50; 4 x 3 pdrs; 2 x 18 inch TT.
Machinery:	Parsons turbines 44,000 hp = 25 knots.
Complement:	800.

[1]September 1908.

ABOVE AND OPPOSITE: *These two pictures were taken soon after the 'Coal Ship' photographs on the preceding pages.* Australia *appears to have left her coaling anchorage and moved up harbour (possibly in the Forth) to secure to a bouy. The cable party are still black from coaling. They are hauling in the picking-up rope on the centre-line capstan to pull the ship up to the bouy so that the anchor cable can be attached. Note the sea-boat (a cutter) with the bouy jumpers aboard standing by the mooring bouy. Deck is still wet from hosing down on completion of 'Coal Ship' (IWM-Q18717 and Q18750). Pictures of* New Zealand *and* Indefatigable *(below) date from soon after Jutland when a light grey scheme with dark panel was adopted.*

New Zealand   IWM—SP874   1916

Indefatigable   *IWM–SP392*   *1916*

ABOVE: The Chaplain conducts prayers at morning divisions aboard Australia at Rosyth in the Forth. Two seamen's divisions, with their divisional officers and midshipmen are seen in the picture. Duty men are rigging a boom in the background. Note the exhaust pipe (right) from the coal stove in one of the messes below (IWM-Q18734).

BELOW: Mealtime on the boy's messdeck in the same ship. Tables could be slung up to the deckhead to give more room in these very congested broadside messdecks (IWM-Q18768).

RIGHT: Flying off a Sopwith 1½ Strutter from one of the midship gun turrets aboard Australia in 1918. The location of the wood flying-off platforms at this period can be seen in the scale drawing on page 23. A 36 ft motor pinnace acts as safety boat. The ship was at anchor at Rosyth. The air-craft, once flown off, had to land ashore after its sortie. (IWM - Q18729).

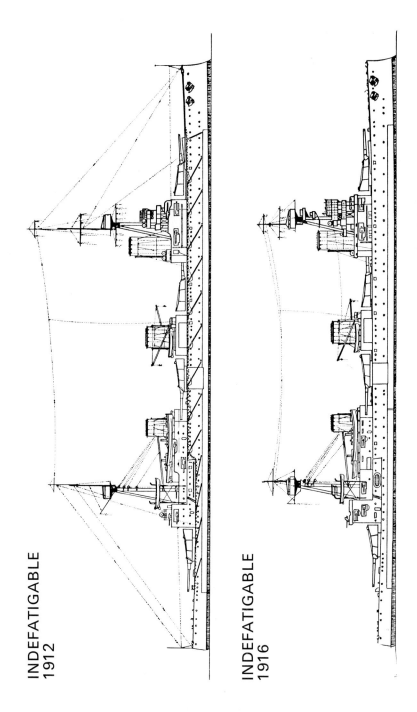

INDEFATIGABLE
1912

INDEFATIGABLE
1916

22

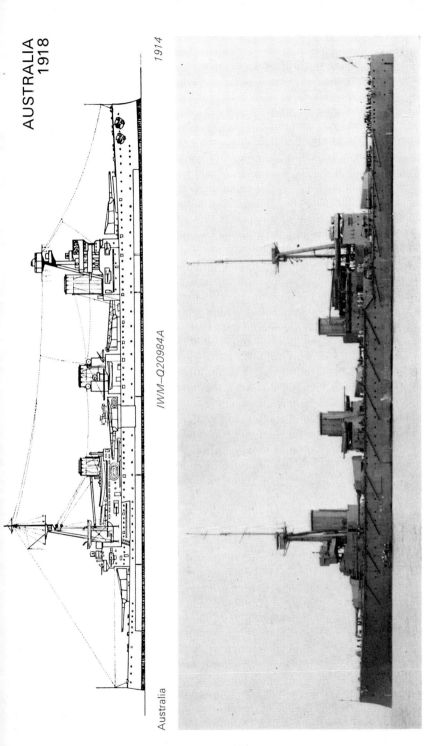

AUSTRALIA
1918

1914

IWM–Q20984A

Australia

23

4: The 'Lion' Class

THE 'Splendid Cats' as these great ships were known with awe and affection enjoyed a tremendous reputation in the service and their gunnery was of a high order. They were notable in many ways when they first appeared being the largest and most expensive (around £2 million) warships built for the Royal Navy.

The adoption of the 13·5 inch gun was on par with the contemporary 'Orion' class battleships but for the first time the tonnage of the battle cruisers exceeded that of the battleships built under the same programme. The reasons for this included the fact that they had been designed to outclass everything the enemy had produced. They had a design speed of 27 knots, and this and those 13·5s again made the battle cruiser concept plausible (until of course the Germans came back again with something better!).

Other features new to battle cruiser design included all centre-line turrets, super-firing ahead and a vastly increased scale of protection. A maximum of 9 inches being achieved with the belt which tapered to 4 inches. Nine inch protection was provided on the turrets and 10 inches on the conning tower. Deck protection was still two inches only and the vunerability of these ships to the effects of plunging fire was still all too obvious. Again despite the enormous increase in cost and size their protection here was still inferior to *Von der Tann* although their vastly superior hitting power was expected to more than compensate.

Again their potential was exaggerated by contemporary journals, their

Lion *(after Jutland)*   IWM–SP1039   1916

Princess Royal　　　　　　　　*IWM—SP2164*　　　　　　　　*1918*

armour being described as of battleship scale and their speed in excess of 34 knots! In fact the *Princess Royal* reached 29½ knots which was impressive enough but they were not the 'ultimate design' which the man in the street thought he had received for his £2 million sterling.

The impression of power and grace they instilled always lent the 'Lions' a certain hauteur and the same ship was herself to gain immortal fame with her exploits as Sir David Beatty's flagship. In all the major actions it was the battle cruisers who were in the thick of the fighting and in the public estimation they gained immense prestige, which made the terrible disasters at Jutland seem all the more tragic.

Ship	Builder	Laid Down	Launched	Completed
Lion	Devonport	29.11.09	6.8.10	5.12
Princess Royal	Vickers	2.5.10	29.4.11	11.12
Queen Mary	Palmers	6.3.11	20.3.12	9.13

Dimensions: 660' (700' OA) x 88' 6" x 26 '5" / 28' 10".
Displacement: 26,350 tons.
Armament: 8 x 13·5 inch/45; 16 x 4 inch/50; 4 x 3 pdrs; 2 x 21 inch TT.
Machinery: Parsons turbines 70,000 hp = 27 knots.
Complement: 997.

25

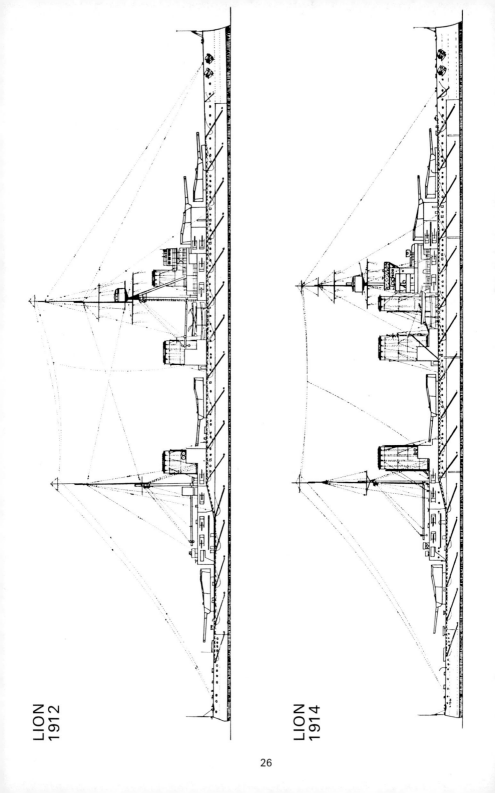

LION
1912

LION
1914

26

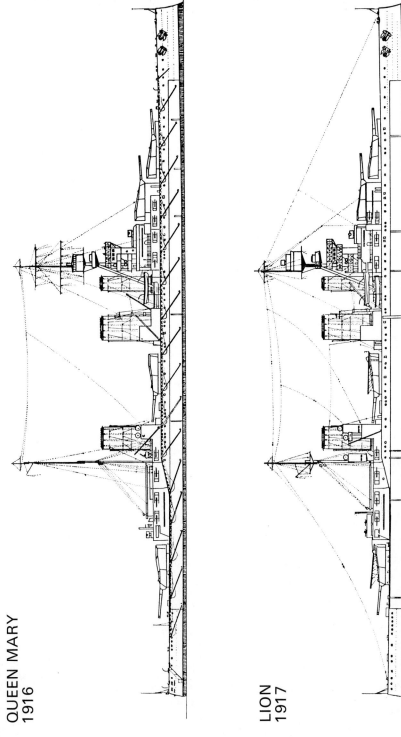

QUEEN MARY
1916

LION
1917

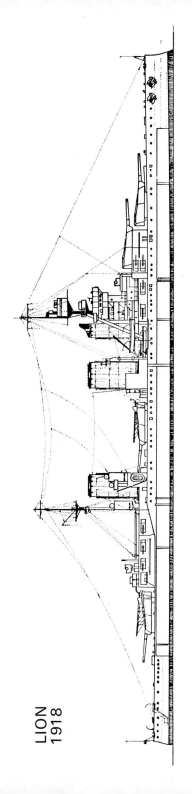

LION
1918

1916

IWM—SP1316

Lion

Queen Mary

IWM–Q21661

1914

Queen Mary

IWM–SP2775

1918

5: The 'Tiger'

INFLUENCED by the design of the Japanese Battle Cruiser *Kongo* which had been ordered from a British yard in 1911, the *Tiger* has been described by many as Britain's most successful and majestic vessel of this type. The more sensible disposition of her turrets, super-firing fore and aft, which was to be the custom with all subsequent capital ships, except the 'Nelson' class, was coupled with the elevation of the secondary battery to 6 inch calibre. Additional armour was worked in over that installed in the 'Lions' which made her the best 'value for money' Battle Cruiser built. She was also the heaviest warship built up to that time and was the last British capital ship to mount the 13·5 inch gun.

Due to the international outlook her building was hurried but appears to have been none the less sturdy for that and as completed she certainly lent beauty and dignity to the Grand Fleet.

'Beside any other she made them look like floating factories. No man who ever served in her fails to recollect her beauty with pride and thankfulness'.*

Although it has been said that she was capable of the impressive speed of 'no less than 35 knots', it is recorded elsewhere that her maximum speed never exceeded 29. Superb as she was, a delight to the eye and of daunting size, her protection still paled when compared with the equivalent German ship, the *Derfflinger*. This vessel showed a 12 inch belt and 8 inch decks against the *Tiger's* 9 inch armour and $2\frac{1}{2}$ inch deck protection.

In the Battle Cruiser as envisaged by Jackie Fisher this would not perhaps have mattered but with the tradition in the Royal Navy of 'engage the enemy more closely', the great ships commanders would no more stand off at a safe range than they would scuttle, and when the test came it was armour, not speed and hitting power, which proved the deciding factor.

Ship	Builder	Laid Down	Launched	Completed
Tiger	John Brown	20.6.12	15.12.13	10.14

Dimensions:	660' (704' OA) x 90' 6" x 28' 5".
Displacement:	28,500 tons.
Armament:	8 x 13·5 inch/45; 12 x 6 inch/45; 4 x 3 pdrs; 4 x 21 inch TT.
Machinery:	Brown Curtiss turbines, 85,000 hp = 28 knots.
	(108,000 hp = 29 knots).
Complement:	1,121.

Years of Endurance (Muir).

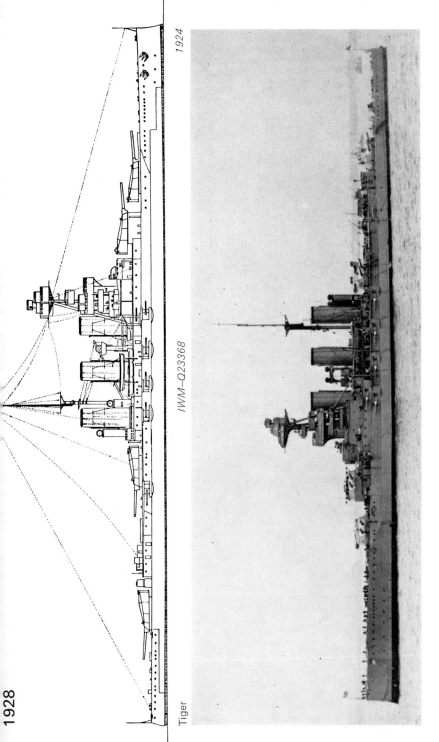

1928

1924

Tiger

6: Beatty

NO work devoted to the story of the Battle Cruiser can be considered complete without a brief outline of their famous leader, with whom the very term Battle Cruiser became synonymous. At a time when the machine appeared to overwhelm the man and warships had reached an awe-inspiring size and complexity, the British public had looked for someone with the Nelson flair of individuality and success. In Sir David Beatty they found the man, and his almost legendary powers were reflected by the exploits of the force he led.

Beatty was born in 1871 of Irish parentage and soon after joining the Royal Navy he first made his mark. As a very young lieutenant he was given command of a gunboat on the Nile. Kitchener was marching through the Sudan to crush the Mahdi's dervishes and avenge the murder of Gordon. Beatty showed dash and enterprise in this naval operation, earning the DSO and also early promotion to the rank of Commander.

He was appointed to the Battleship *Barfleur* on the China Station and shortly after he arrived to take up his new position the Boxer rebellion broke out. Beatty managed to get himself involved with a landing party sent by Sir Edward Seymour to relieve the beleagured Legations at Peking (Jellicoe was also present). Beatty again distinguished himself in the subsequent fighting during which he was badly wounded. A result of his gallantry was his promotion in 1900, to Captain, over the heads of 219 more senior commanders, which earned him more enemies than friends.

Marriage to an American heiress was followed by further sea-going appointments in cruisers and by 1909 he had reached the top of the captains' list in command of the battleship *Queen.*

His dazzling rise and good fortune did not stop there for in January 1911 he was promoted to Rear-Admiral at the age of 38, the regulations barring him from such a promotion with less than six years as a Captain behind him, being specially waived. He accepted his good fortune but with his usual individuality shocked the service by turning down an appointment in the Atlantic Fleet.

Instead he sought, and received, an interview with Winston Churchill who had recently taken over the post of First Lord of the Admiralty. Success attracts success and the two men saw eye to eye on many aspects. Churchill offered Beatty the post of Naval Secretary against the advice of many senior officers and the young Admiral's future was thereby assured under Churchill's patronage.

His appointment to command of the Battle Cruiser Squadron, recently formed, came in 1913 and he took over from its first commander, Admiral Sir Lewis Bayley, another 'fire-eater'. On assuming command he found that no formal policy had been laid down for the operations of these mighty vessels in time of war and he therefore set to and made his own.

To a straightforward 'fighting' sailor like Beatty the principles were obvious. As the spearhead of the Fleet his ships had two major functions. The first was as a powerful scouting force to seek out the enemy. The second followed naturally upon the first; once the enemy main Fleet was sighted it

Invincible

Lion

Princess Royal

Indefatigable

These were unofficial badges, mostly devised by members of the crews; after 1918 official badges were adopted and —in surviving ships —this meant a change.

must be lured towards the main British Fleet which would then destroy it.

Supplementary duties which fell into his command's sphere of operations included supporting light cruiser forces, and the provision of a fast flank wing to the main Battle Fleet in a general action.

His principal functions decided, Beatty turned to training his command for the task ahead. His premier task was the destruction of the Battle Cruisers in the German Fleet, and any action fought between these ships was necessarily to be an affair of high speed and long-range firing. As the British Fleet had never fired its guns in practise at a target towed at more than six knots the gunners were woefully unprepared for this type of action. Beatty's answer was to practise these tactics until his gunners became probably the most accurate in any fleet.

Filson Young's invaluable record* includes a descriptive passage of the first such test held in June 1913 in the North Sea;

'The *Indomitable* had been sent off in advance to a point a hundred miles out in the North Sea whence she was to return at full speed towards the English coast, the other Battle Cruisers meanwhile spreading in order to locate her and bring her to action. Steam for four-fifths speed had been ordered in the whole squadron, which then scattered and searched the sea for their objective. The dark smudge of smoke on the horizon, which is the first visual intimation of friend or foe alike, was located; the squadron formed into line ahead and stormed through the smooth waters towards the *Indomitable.* The organisation which controls the firing of the guns was kept busy, for although the guns were not fired, the whole intricate routine by which the ranges and bearings telephoned constantly down to the transmitting station in the bowels of the ship, are worked out and signalled up to the turrets in terms of opening or closing ranges, was gone through. Never before had the crews of heavy guns had such an experience; for the speed at which we and the *Indomitable* were steaming towards each other gave a closing rate of something approaching a mile a minute, and the distance of fifteen miles, at which the enemy was first sighted, was demolished in seventeen minutes, after which the exercise was over'.

Not at all unusual nowadays, but this was the *first time* it had been done and Beatty ensured it was not the last. August 1914 saw him flying his flag in the *Lion* with the *Queen Mary* and *New Zealand.* The *Princess Royal,* though nominally a part of his squadron, was out in the Atlantic on one of the fruitless missions which these ships were initially given due to the lack of official policy.

Beatty's war service was outstanding and his dashing leadership ensured that the Battle Cruisers were always in the thick of the fighting. With his distinctive style of dress, the cap raked down over one eye and the six-button monkey jacket, he became identified with the best qualities of the Royal Navy, aggressiveness and fearlessness.

He certainly always sought combat and was in no doubt whatsoever of his duty on sighting the enemy; this was to either destroy him or lead him to destruction. Although his handling of events at Jutland has received severe judgement from his numerous critics he was seen by many to be the man who would deliver victory if it were possible.

He can hardly be blamed for the defects of his ships and until Jutland

---

*With the Battle Cruisers, Filson Young (Cassel, 1921).

Admiral Beatty in characteristic pose, wearing his famous six-button jacket which was not strictly in accord with dress regulations — it should have had eight buttons (IWM-Q19571).

he always had faith that their gunnery would decide the issue. Only bad luck prevented him from destroying his opponents at Dogger Bank and he most certainly saved the day at Heligoland Bight.

'Where was Beatty?', asks a modern historian when examining the Battle of Jutland. Beatty was in fact doing his job. He had pressed home his attack on the German Scouting Fleet with courage and determination. Even after the completely unexpected destruction of two of his own ships, he had contacted the main enemy fleet and as was the policy, his policy, he turned and led them to the Commander-in-Chief. This was the only sane thing to do when confronted with 16 battleships against his remaining force.

Likewise, the gallant Admiral Hood on sighting the enemy fleet, took his ships without hesitation, and at high speed, *towards* them and engaged. It cannot be said that the Battle Cruiser Force allowed the High Seas Fleet to escape that May day, for their immediate actions were to *close* with the enemy.

Eventually Beatty replaced Jellicoe in command of the Grand Fleet and made changes in the rigid fighting instructions. He was not to get the opportunity to put his ideas into effect but was rewarded with the superb spectacle of the surrender of the High Seas Fleet in November 1918, a fitting climax to his wartime service.

A year later he became First Sea Lord and embarked on a long hard struggle to prevent political considerations reducing the Royal Navy below the 'safe' limits he insisted on. This was one fight that Beatty lost, but the nation should be grateful to him for without his determined efforts things would have been even more grim in the post-1922 Fleet than they were. 'The whole future of the Empire rests on this question', he wrote in 1921, about the new construction programme then under attack at home, and he was right.

*'He had struggled with might and main for seven years against a wave of misguided idealism which engulfed Whitehall during the post-war era; he had not hesitated to throw the whole weight of his great professional experience and high office into the scales to prevent surrender to the

British Sea Power, Admiral B.B. Schofield (Batsford, 1962).

35

penurious promptings of the Treasury and the pressures of international politics'.

But in the end the politicians had their way and the nation paid the inevitable price 18 years later. Beatty himself died before his forebodings came to pass, in March 1936, and was buried in St Paul's Cathedral. His bust now stands in Trafalgar Square alongside Jellicoe and beneath the shadow of Nelson's Column.

Beatty did not design or build his Battle Cruisers; he merely trained and commanded their crews to fight, and fight magnificently, at every opportunity. It was unfortunate that with these ships, 'Gallant leadership only proved their weakness'.

7: The 'Renown' Class

DESPITE all the misgivings in many quarters about the role, cost and vulnerability of the Battle Cruiser, the start of hostilities in 1914 produced, in the actions of Heligoland Bight and the Falklands, immediate and outstanding justification of the type, and served to confirm Admiral Fisher's apparent foresight. Because the 1914 battleship construction programme had been held up Fisher sought, and gained, permission to re-designate two of the contemplated Royal Sovereign class battleships as battle cruisers.

His preoccupation with the 'Baltic Project' coupled with his undiminished faith in ships with high speed and heavy guns was to result in the construction of a whole specialised fleet of shallow draught lightly-armoured vessels, of which the *Renown* and *Repulse* were the only two to survive with their major features intact.

Again, armour protection went by the board and was only on the same small scale as the earlier *Indefatigable*, but an enormous increase in displacement and length was demanded in the requirement of a vessel able to carry six of the new 15 inch guns at speeds of over 32 knots. As a result, when these ships finally appeared shortly after Jutland, they were regarded with scorn in the fleet. Fisher also specified that these vessels were to be completed at high speed and both ships took under two years to get to sea. The 'tissue paper' protection was so obviously inadequate and the prevailing mood in the fleet after Jutland so adverse to this type of 'suicide' that both ships immediately were taken in hand and extra deck plating was worked into them, but the

ABOVE: Renown *as she appeared in 1922, dressed overall at sea while* carrying HRH The Prince of Wales on his world tour (painting by Tom Stone).

BELOW: Two of the unofficial ships' badges, for Repulse *and* Renown (Arthur North).

The old and the new. The 'Lion' class (right) compared with a 'Renown' class ship in 1918 (IWM-SP2780).

belt of inadequate waist armour had to remain as it was for the duration of hostilities.

Another unfortunate experiment, which never really worked out to any satisfaction, was the adoption of the triple 4 inch gun as secondary armament.

On the very limited credit side was the fact that they were by far the fastest capital ships yet built for any navy and they incorporated one feature soon to be universally adopted, the bulged hull as an integral part of the ship instead of a 'tacked-on' afterthought.

Their frequent visits to the dockyards earned them the nicknames of 'Refit' and 'Repair' at Scapa Flow and that they survived the war was probably more due to lack of action than anything else. Although 'tin cans' in terms of modern capital ship construction their age and speed proved their salvation after the war when far superior ships went to the breakers. Their reconstruction merits a separate section later in this book.

Ship	Builder	Laid Down	Launched	Completed
Renown	Fairfield	25.1.15	4.3.16	20.9.16
Repulse	John Brown	25.1.15	8.1.16	18.8.16

Dimensions:	750' (794' OA) x 90' x 25' 4" (27').
Displacement:	27,500 tons. (average).
Armament:	6 x 15 inch; 17 x 4 inch; 2 x 3 inch; 2 x 21 inch TT.
Machinery:	Brown Curtiss turbines 112,000 = 30 knots.
	(120,000 = 32 knots).
Complement:	967.

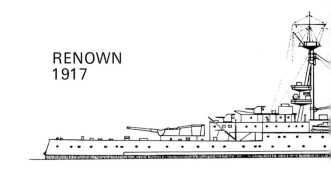

RENOWN
1917

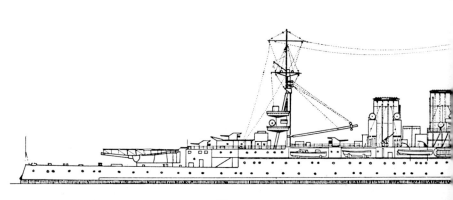

Repulse   *IWM–SP2186*   *1918*

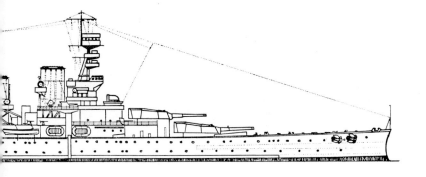

**RENOWN
1919**

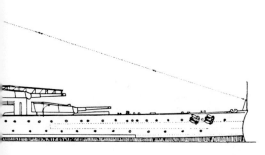

Renown   *IWM–SP1776*   *1918*
(Note triple 4 inch gun mounts)

Repulse   *IWM–SP1085*   *1917*

RIGHT:A detailed view of the 'fighting top' in Repulse *with the main range finder/director tower at the top.*

Indomitable

Queen Mary

New Zealand

Inflexible

These were unofficial badges devised aboard ship and replaced later—in some surviving ships—by official badges.

Glorious   *IWM–SP2615*   *1918*

8: The 'Courageous' Class

THIS unique pair of ships, together with their half-sister, *Furious,* were yet further examples of the 'Baltic Plan' which Fisher pursued with some vigour before his abrupt departure from the Admiralty over the Dardenelles operation, which he opposed. Quite why his beloved dictum of 'big guns and high speed' should have such prominence in a programme basically designed to support a military landing is not clear. Certainly for such an invasion monitors would have done the job of support fireships as well and at less cost.

As it was these *Courageous* class ships were completed very quickly but joined the Grand Fleet instead, for the Baltic Plan faded away with Fisher's departure from office.

To get the necessary money voted for their construction they had been designated as 'large light cruisers', a delightful piece of deception in the face of an intransigent government, (not repeated until the classification of the 'Hunt' class destroyers as 'escort vessels' in the face of similar circumstances in the late 1930s).

Although virtually unarmoured and of shallow draught, their size and armament placed them naturally under the battle cruiser classification. Adopting the twin 15 inch gun mounting, which was to prove such a success, their

speed requirements and draught necessitated the cutting down of the number of guns to four. Other similarities to the Renowns were the adoption of the triple 4 inch mounting as secondary armament. Their turbines were fully geared and, for the first time, in ships of this size, the boilers were of the small-bore type.

Of little or no practical value to the Grand Fleet they nevertheless saw employment with that force under the guise of the 1st Cruiser Squadron, but were out-fought by German light cruisers without their superior speed and long-range armament creating the perfect situation it had always been held to guarantee. This little-known action should have finally condemned the battle cruiser concept, but their construction continued nevertheless! Indeed Fisher had visions of a new ultimate in this type, HMS *Incomparable,* some 900 ft long mounting 20 inch guns!

The *Furious* set the stage with a jump in armament to 18 inch calibre. She was designed to mount two of these, and as such would have presented some interest but she was never completed as a battle cruiser. The monster gun was too much for her frail hull and when fired the shower of rivets down below is said to have resembled snow! She saw some limited service as a seaplane tender before being fully converted to an aircraft-carrier, but as such she has no further place in our story. The Grand Fleet knew the trio as the 'Curious', 'Outrageous' and 'Spurious' in service.

Ship	Builder	Laid Down	Launched	Completed
Courageous	Elswick	3.15	5.2.16	1.17
Glorious	Harland & Wolff.	5.15	20.4.16	1.17

Dimensions:	735' (786' OA) x 81' x 23' 5".
Displacement:	18,600 tons.
Armament:	4 x 15 inch; 18 x 4 inch; 2 x 3 inch; 2 x 21 inch TT.
Machinery:	Parsons turbines, 90,000 = 31 knots.
Complement:	835 (average).

(Scale drawings on next page)

Courageous *and* Glorious *are here shown at sea in 1918 as the 1st Cruiser Squadron. Note kite balloon flying from* Glorious. *A 'W' class destroyer is between them as escort (IWM-SP727).*

COURAGEOUS
1916

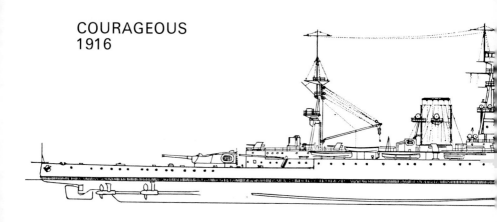

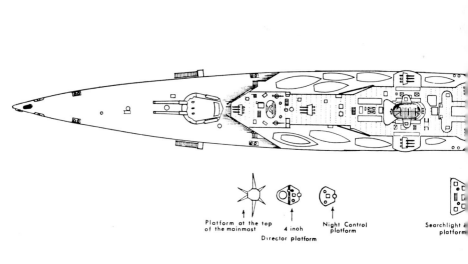

Platform at the top
of the mainmast

4 inch
Director platform

Night Control
platform

Searchlight
platform

GLORIOUS
1916

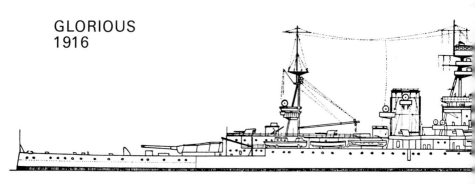

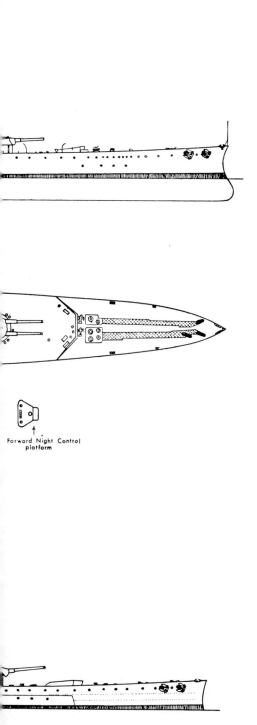

Forward Night Control
platform

Early 1917

IWM–SP206

Glorious (*on builder's trials*)

9: The Battle Cruiser at War

THESE vessels took a leading part in every major action at sea in the Great War and in a book of this size it is obviously not possible to write in great detail of each action. However, the principal dispositions and engagements are clearly of interest and for the movements of individual ships reference should be made to the class notes.

On the outbreak of war in August 1914 the Battle Cruisers were on station as follows:

1st Battle Cruiser Squadron, (Vice-Admiral Sir David Beatty):
Lion (Flag) (Captain A. E. Chatfield, CVO).
Princess Royal (Captain O. de B. Brock, ADC).
Queen Mary (Captain W. R. Hall).
New Zealand (Captain Lionel Halsey CMG).
This squadron was with the Grand Fleet.

2nd Battle Cruiser Squadron:
Inflexible (Flag) (Captain A. N. Loxley).
Indefatigable (Captain C. F. Sowerby).
Indomitable (Captain F. W. Kennedy).
This squadron was under the command of the Commander-in-Chief Mediterranean Fleet, Admiral Sir A. Berkeley Milne, Bart, GCVO.

Of the other vessels, *Invincible* was to join the 1st BCS, *Australia* was Flagship of the Australian Navy and was in Pacific waters, and the *Tiger* was still being completed.

The Furious *was originally designed as a half-sister to* Courageous *and* Glorious, *differing mainly in having two 18 inch gun turrets instead of 15 inch turrets. Proving unsuccessful with these huge guns she was soon converted to an aircraft carrier with a full flying-off deck forward and the forward 18 inch turret suppressed. This 1918 view shows the Sopwith 1½ Strutters ranged on deck (behind the palisades) and the forward derricks which were used to hoist seaplanes in and out.* Furious *was no longer rated as a battle cruiser in this form but she is shown here for comparison with the scale drawings of the other two ships on the preceding pages. Later all three ships were converted to full flat-top aircraft carriers and were in service as such in 1939 (MoD-Fleet Air Arm).*

THE ESCAPE OF THE GOEBEN (AUGUST 2 - 10 1914)

The vulnerability of the French troop transports in the western Mediterranean weighed very heavily on the Admiralty as the last days of peace slipped away, for although the French could deploy a strong naval force in that area they had no ship which could equal the German battle cruiser *Goeben,* (22,640 tons, 10 x 11 inch guns, 29 knots). The British and French navies had no official policy for combined action in the area and so it was deemed wisest that the German squadron, (*Goeben* was accompanied by the cruiser, *Breslau*), should be kept under close observation by at least two of the British battle cruisers which Admiral Milne had at his disposal.

Accordingly on August 4 the *Indomitable* and *Indefatigable* duly sighted the German vessel and shadowed her. They were instructed that should she attempt to attack French transports she was to be engaged, this despite the fact that the British ultimatum on the declaration of war had not expired. This decision was soon reversed and the Commander-in-Chief Mediterranean received a further communication instructing that until the declaration of war his ships were to keep off the *Goeben.*

All that day the two British ships tailed the German vessel. She was in easy range and potentially completely outgunned. As it was she patiently waited until nightfall and then by virtue of her superior speed quickly drew away and was lost to them. Admiral Milne had sailed from Malta at midnight with the hostilities now officially opened and concentrated his three big ships

47

WILLS'S CIGARETTES.

WILLS'S CIGARETTES.

BADGE.

BADGE.

VENTIS SECUNDIS.

QUI TANGIT FRANGATUR.

MOTTO.

MOTTO.

The official badges for Hood *and* Repulse *adopted in the 1920s (from the cigarette card set 'Ships Badges', reproduced courtesy Imperial Tobacco Co.).*

with two light cruisers off Pantellaria.

Goeben meanwhile had put into Messina and with *Breslau* began a hasty and complete coaling which lasted until 6 August. While there the German Admiral Souchon received orders to proceed to Constantinople in readiness for the declared alliance between Germany and Turkey. Therefore while British eyes were on the Western basin or the Adriatic the German squadron was fully prepared for a high speed dash to the east.

Acting under his previous orders to protect the French transports Admiral Milne cruised with his heavy ships to the west of Sicily while the *Indomitable* coaled at Bizerta. Thus when Souchon finally sailed from Messina at 5 pm with decks cleared for a major action with at least two of the British Battle Cruisers he found that his course to the south was clear. Still in a position to intercept the German ships were the armoured cruisers of Rear-Admiral Troubridge. These ships, *Black Prince, Defence, Duke of Edinburgh* and *Warrior* were 14,000 ton vessels with 9·2 inch main armaments, and as such were clearly inferior, individually, to the *Goeben,* but there were four of them and in addition they had in company eight destroyers.

It had been assumed that if she turned east from Italy the *Goeben* would try to make the port of Pola and the safety of the Adriatic coast of Austro-Hungary. Troubridge initially received no orders to intercept but took his squadron south none the less. Reinforcements in the form of the cruiser *Dublin* and two destroyers were steaming from Malta to join him and with a force of fifteen vessels it seemed possible that the *Goeben* must be intercepted. However, Troubridge had decided that the German battle cruiser with her 11 inch guns would constitute a superior force and that his whole squadron would have been picked off while still out of range. Accordingly he turned back to guard the Adriatic. The *Goeben* proceeded unchecked.

The three British battle cruisers eventually followed the German ship eastward but at a dawdling pace and thus although the *Goeben* delayed a further 36 hours in the Aegean trying to establish the Turkish position she was never brought to battle and the strategic implications of her arrival in the Black Sea were tragic and immense.

THE BATTLE OF THE 'BIGHT (AUGUST 28 1914)

With a view to interrupting the serenity of the German naval positions around the fortified island of Heligoland a raid in force was planned involving eight submarines of Commander Keyes' force and the Harwich force of light cruisers and destroyers of Sir Reginald Tyrwhitt. The plan was for the submarines and destroyers under Keyes to lure out the patrols and for Tyrwhitt to go in behind and destroy them. Should the Germans rise to the bait with heavier metal, then Sir David Beatty was on call to the north with the 1st Battle Cruiser Squadron. The plan was daring and simple, in practice it was to prove successful.

Tyrwhitt with the *Arethusa, Fearless* and destroyers of 1st and 3rd Destroyer Flotillas reached their pre-arranged positions at first light on August 28, and immediately the British destroyers were in contact with German patrols, rapidly driving them back to seek greater protection. The German light cruiser *Frauenlob* appeared and engaged the brand new *Arethusa* causing her severe casualties and damage before the *Fearless* and destroyers diverted her attention. The plan was obviously going awry and developed into a general scramble in and out of the mist between the light forces on both sides.

It soon became apparent that the Germans were bringing up cruiser reinforcements and the predicament of the crippled *Arethusa* was obvious. Although the big German destroyer *V187* and several smaller units had been sunk the cruisers *Mainz, Köln, Stettin, Frauenlob* and *Ariadne* all began to intervene and the British found themselves hard pressed. To Beatty, some ten miles to the west, the picture formed was a confused one, but one thing was obvious, the battle had been in progress for almost four hours and the British force was in considerable danger.

Without further delay the 1st Battle Cruiser Squadron, risking the submarine dangers, and minefields, swung round at 1130 hours and proceeded at full speed to the assistance of Tyrwhitt's force. The *Lion, Queen Mary, Princess Royal, New Zealand* and *Invincible* were going into action in one of their original roles, to clear up enemy cruiser forces, but with the Jade river so close and the High Seas Fleet raising steam they could have equally encountered the cruisers of Scheer or Hipper.

First on the scene were Commander Goodenough's light cruisers and they quickly helped despatch the damaged German *Mainz,* but even so the *Köln, Ariadne, Stralsund* and *Stettin* were closing around the British force while the destroyers were fully engaged with yet another, the *Strassburg.* It was at this perilous moment that the battle cruisers arrived.

> 'Once more the situation was fraught with grave danger. Then, quite suddenly, the shape of a very large ship loomed out the murk to the westward. She was steaming at full speed, the smoke rolling from her funnels and the white bow wave piled up round her sharp stem. One by one four more huge hulls came into view astern of her'.*

---

*With the Battle Cruisers, Filson Young (Cassel, 1921).

Thanks to Beatty the situation was now reversed and the German cruisers now felt the might of the 13·5 inch and 12 inch shells of the big ships for the first time. The first German vessel brought under fire by a British Battle Cruiser was the light cruiser *Köln*. She was sighted from *Lion's* bridge to port at high speed steaming north-east. Both the flagship and the next astern, *Princess Royal* engaged her with salvoes for a few brief minutes. Her engines demolished, she was saved from immediate destruction by one of her compatriots.

This unfortunate was the *Ariadne* which went across the bows of the British squadron on a south-east course at point blank range. Although steaming hard she was caught fair and square in a deluge of heavy shells. Ablaze from end to end and with a heavy list and over one hundred dead or dying she was left to sink.

At 0110 hours Beatty, having penetrated to within 32 miles of the High Seas Fleet anchorage signalled the 'Retirement' and on the way out the *Lion* came across the damaged *Köln* and at 3,500 yards range sent her to the bottom with three controlled salvoes, taking over 500 of her crew with her.

The German casualties amounted to three light cruisers and a destroyer while the British had the *Arethusa* and two destroyers badly damaged. There is no doubt that it was Beatty's intervention which tipped the scales and turned a possible defeat into a significant victory. The Kaiser was dismayed and Churchill compared this victory with the hypothetical case of German destroyers breaking into the Solent and their battle cruisers penetrating as far as the Nab. Such was the achievement of Beatty's command.

There was much that was shown to be wrong with British naval thinking at the battle of the Bight, mainly the slowness in which complicated changes of orders were communicated, or rather, not communicated, to the men on the spot, but leadership was not lacking on the field of battle itself. Opponents of Beatty have remarked that his intervention in the nick of time was over-dramatised and produced hero worship. Beatty, it has been said did nothing to discourage it. However, it is on record that when the 1st Battle Cruiser Squadron returned to Scapa Flow and were met by cheering crews on the battleships Beatty was very angry. 'He did *not* consider the sinking of a few small ships by battle cruisers a matter for Fleet cheering'.*

THE BATTLE OF THE FALKLAND ISLANDS (DECEMBER 8 1914)

The most powerful German force still at large towards the end of 1914 was Admiral von Spee's Pacific squadron, which consisted of the two powerful armoured cruisers *Scharnhorst* and *Gneisenau,* (11,600 tons, 8 x 9·2 inch guns, 22 knots). These had crossed the Pacific, evading the searches made by the *Australia* and Japanese forces and had defeated Admiral Cradock's force of similar but older vessels at the battle of Coronel. In company with the fast light cruisers *Leipzig, Nurnberg* and *Dresden* they had disappeared into the wastes of water off South America and could appear anywhere on the vulnerable trade routes with disastrous effect. To remedy this situation stern measures were put in hand by the Admiralty.

Under the command of Vice-Admiral Sir Doveton Sturdee, the *Invincible* and *Inflexible* sailed from home waters on November 11 in strict secrecy. By December 7 they had arrived at the Falkland Islands, having meanwhile made contact with the cruisers *Caernarvon, Kent, Cornwall, Bristol,* and the *Glasgow* which had survived Coronel by virtue of her speed. Also at Port Stanley was the old battleship *Canopus* being used as a battery. An attack by the strong German squadron was expected and the British ships immediately began coaling.

*op cit.

Battle of the Falkland Islands, December 8, 1914. The Inflexible *opens fire at the enemy about 1 pm. This picture was taken from the maintop of* Invincible *by Paymaster Sub-Lieutenant A. D. Duckworth (IWM-Q20891).*

Fate was on their side for the very next day von Spee appeared over the horizon and was fired on by *Canopus.* On sighting the tripods of the two battle cruisers the Germans realised that they were doomed. The day was clear, the British had the whole of it to catch and fight the German squadron. Spee made off at his best speed and scattered his cruisers to save themselves while he prepared to draw off the British forces, but it was to no avail. Only the *Dresden* escaped but respite was brief for she was cornered three months later.

While the Germans hurried off to the west the British battle cruisers sailed

The Invincible *pictured from the bridge of the cruiser* Caernarvon *during the Falkland Islands battle (IWM-SP2093).*

as soon as they were ready. In all it was two hours after the first sightings before the *Invincible* and *Inflexible* left Port Stanley by which time the Germans were fifteen miles ahead, hull down over the horizon. Sturdee was unperturbed however, and at a steady 20 knots he gradually overhauled them. Soon after 1300 hours *Inflexible* opened the action by engaging the unfortunate *Leipzig*, which had fallen behind her compatriots. *Scharnhorst* and *Gneisenau*, in a vain attempt to close the range came under the concentrated fire of the two British Battle Cruisers, which were able to choose their own distance exactly as Fisher had intended that they should.

Some proof of the appalling standard of shooting which prevailed even in 1914 can be had from the length of time that this unequal contest continued. It was not until 1545 hours that the *Scharnhorst* turned turtle and went down with her Admiral and his whole crew, while the *Gneisenau* followed her sister a few hours later. When they eventually went down the *Inflexible* had only 30 and the *Invincible* only 32 rounds remaining for each of their main armament guns.

The almost complete destruction of von Spee's force meant that, save for one or two isolated cruisers, the entire German Navy was now bottled up in the North Sea and completely unable to intervene in the oceans of the world. They tried several times to use their fleet to seek a solution to this *impasse,* but on each occasion were driven back by the superior numbers of the Grand Fleet. By 1917 they had turned to the submarine to dispute control of the British sea routes, but far too late. The supremacy of Britain's naval power had, by the end of 1914, already laid the fate of German hopes and aspirations.

THE GERMAN RAIDS (DECEMBER 16 1914)

As if stung into a realisation of their impotence the Germans staged a series of hit-and-run raids on English coastal towns of no military significance during the latter part of December 1914 and early in 1915. Hipper's Battle Cruisers and light cruisers, the famed Scouting Group, dashed across the North Sea and on November 3 fired several salvoes of 11 inch and 12 inch shells into the beach at Great Yarmouth in Norfolk and then fled. The use of such powerful ships against a defenceless town earned Hipper the derisive name of 'baby-killer' in England, but the true purpose of the attacks was to persuade the Admiralty to divide its forces, and in this they were successful.

Intelligence gave early warning of another such raid and in anticipation the 2nd Battle Squadron, the Harwich cruisers and Beatty's Battle Cruisers sailed to rendezvous in the area of the Dogger Bank, to be in a position to intercept. Hipper indeed sailed and early on the morning of December 16 his huge ships appeared off the English coast again, inside the protective minefields. While *Seydlitz, Moltke* and *Blücher* pumped heavy shells into Hartlepool, the *Derfflinger* and *Von der Tann* did likewise to Scarborough and the cruiser *Kolberg* laid a minefield.

Thanks to the Intelligence warnings the Germans were in fact trapped for both Beatty and Warrender were to the seaward of them. But unknown to the British at the time was the fact that the bulk of the High Seas Fleet was also at sea in support of Hipper. Fleeting contact between the cruiser screens of Beatty and Ingenhol resulted in the abrupt cessation of the German sortie and they hurriedly put about, fearing Jellicoe's battleships were on the scene.

When the news of the bombardment came at 0852 Beatty's force had only just learnt of the presence of enemy cruisers in the vicinity. The only seven destroyers available to him had been in contact with the German cruiser *Roon* and Beatty had been told by Warrender, commanding the 2nd Battle Squadron, that this vessel and five destroyers were to the east. At 0852 however, Beatty swung his ships, *Lion, Princess Royal, Tiger* and *New Zealand,* to the west to block the escape route opposite Whitby. The German ships had already combined and delivered a brief bombardment on this town before steering a rapid course eastward.

At this time, around 1130 hours, the weather came down as it does so quickly in the North Sea, with heavy driving rain squalls and mist, and although the cruiser wings of Commander Goodenough were in sporadic contact with the enemy, Hipper drove past through the closing trap and escaped unscathed. Impressed with their good fortune they tried the same tactics again, but the third time was not so lucky and at Dogger Bank the German battle cruisers came very close to total destruction.

THE BATTLE OF THE DOGGER BANK (JANUARY 24 1915)

This time Hipper came out with the *Seydlitz* (Flag), *Moltke, Derfflinger* and *Blücher,* with four light cruisers and a destroyer flotilla, their objective being the destruction of British fishing craft off the Dogger Bank. Some would feel these an even lesser target than Whitby, but to the Germans they were a worthwhile target for such vessels.

Again Admiralty Intelligence got wind of the foray and once more Tyrwhitt's well tried Harwich force sailed to rendezvous with the heavy squadrons coming down from the north, Vice-Admiral Bradford with the 3rd Battle Squadron and Beatty with the *Lion, Tiger, Princess Royal* (*Queen Mary,* noted for her gunnery, was refitting) of the 1st Battle Cruiser Squadron, and *New Zealand,* (Flag) and *Indomitable* of the 2nd Battle Cruiser Squadron which had just been formed, (although many felt that lack of ships at that particular time did not warrant it).

Just after dawn on January 24 the *Aurora* of Tyrwhitt's force became engaged with the German cruiser *Kolberg,* leading Hipper's ships. Beatty at once sent Goodenough's cruiser screen in to make contact and altered course towards the gun flashes. At 0747 the *Southampton* signalled the long awaited news, 'Enemy sighted are 4 battle cruisers, speed 24 knots'. It was indeed the elusive Hipper at long last but at the first contact he had turned his force about and was flying at his best speed to safety. With the enemy appearing as 'four separate wedges or triangles of smoke' on the eastern horizon it was clearly to be a long stern chase and the British ships gradually worked their speed up in pursuit. At 0810 speed was given for 24 knots, at 0815 this was increased to 25. This was still not enough and at 0834 the signal went down the racing line of giants for 27 knots.

The *Indomitable* at the rear of the British line had a maximum top speed of 25 knots but during the long chase managed to get a record 26, but even so she began to fall behind. Likewise on the German side the unfortunate *Blücher* lacked both the speed and armour, and, as each British vessel in turn brought her into range, she received the brunt of the attack.

The rear of Hipper's line opened fire at 0844 but were still short of range. Nevertheless they continued firing at intervals as the range came steadily down. Some eight minutes later the *Lion* commenced firing at 22,000 yards with a sighting shot from 'B' turret and for the first time the Battle Cruisers of Germany and Britain were engaged in combat.

Beatty signalled for 29 knots, which although beyond the capacity of most of his force gave them a spur and the huge vessels were now rushing through the tumbling grey water. The *New Zealand* and *Indomitable* were now falling further behind but Beatty signalled, 'Well done *Indomitable*,' in recognition of the sterling efforts her stokers were now making.

At 0905 hours the *Lion* ordered her companions to engage the enemy and four minutes later the first 13·5 inch shell from the British flagship crashed into the unfortunate *Blücher*. The *Tiger*, next astern, had not long joined the force and was not properly worked up. Her gunnery therefore left something to be desired and *Queen Mary* was doubly missed, nevertheless she commenced firing at 0920 hours whereupon the *Lion* shifted target to the *Moltke*.

The ranges had now come down to 18,000 yards and the rear three German ships were concentrating their fire on the *Lion*. Not surprisingly, at 0928 she was hit, though not seriously. In order to split the enemy fire Beatty ordered his ships in range to 'Engage corresponding ship in line', and in accordance with this *Lion* engaged the *Seydlitz*, *Princess Royal* exchanged fire with the *Moltke*, and the *New Zealand*, coming into range gave the now fatally crippled *Blücher* her attention. Unfortunately the *Tiger* also concentrated on the *Seydlitz* which then left the powerful *Derfflinger* to make uninterrupted attacks on the gallant *Lion* at the head of the line.

Despite this the Germans were hard pressed and at 0940 *Lion* landed a devastating blow on Hipper's flagship. From the *Seydlitz* came the dull glowing and fading glare which marked the penetration and explosion of a shell, as a 13·5 inch projectile pierced through the armoured barbette of her after turret. Exploding in the reloading chamber of this turret it ignited the cordite charges and in an instant the flames leapt into the turret itself cremating its crew. It also spread in a flash through the ammunition chamber where the crew in a vain attempt at escape were passing through to the fore turret. Also killing these unfortunates the flash then engulfed the second turret. Admiral Scheer later stated that, 'The flames rose above the turrets as high as a house'. The after magazines were quickly flooded which saved the ship, but she was badly damaged.

At 0949 *Lion* was hit hard in return, an 11 inch shell penetrating her 4 inch magazine trunk, but it failed to explode. But at 1018 she shook from a very severe blow, which led many to think that she had been torpedoed. In fact it was two waterline hits from the 12 inch guns of *Derfflinger*. Her armour plate was driven in and the feed-water tank of the port condenser was pierced. This was ultimately to put her port engine out of action, though for the moment she held her place in the van. Beatty made the signal at 1028 to 'Form a line of bearing NNW and proceed at your utmost speed', in order that the range should be closed on the fleeing enemy as quickly as possible and the issue decided. Enemy salvoes kept arriving, and with two or more ships concentrating on her it is not surprising that *Lion* should have been hit and hit again. The most dangerous moment came at 1041 hours when a shell ignited the charges in 'A' turret magazine. Only quick flooding of the magazine prevented her from blowing up.

By 1107 hours the *Lion* was forced to fall out of line as her engines faltered and her speed dropped to 15 knots. It was clearly still within the power of the remaining ships, all mainly untouched, to effect the destruction of the German squadron. The *Blücher* was obviously doomed, and the *Indomitable* had been ordered to finish her off.

At 1102 hours Beatty had made the signal, 'Course NE', in order to place the British ships between the sinking *Blücher* and the other German ships, while at the same time ensuring that *Princess Royal* and *Tiger* would still maintain close contact. To make quite certain that his intentions were known as the squadron swept by the limping flagship, Beatty sent two further signals, at 1105, 'Attack the rear of the enemy' and at 1107, 'Keep nearer to the enemy'.

Unfortunately Admiral Moore read the two signals, of 1102 and 1105, in conjunction and took it to mean that his ships should concentrate on the *Blücher*. This was an unfortunate interpretation for it enabled the damaged *Seydlitz* and her companions to make good their escape while all the ground made up in the last hour's chase was thrown away. By the time Beatty had rejoined the squadron in the destroyer *Attack* it was too late, Hipper had been reprieved again.

The *Blücher* went down soon afterwards but the destruction of this outclassed vessel and the heavy damage to *Seydlitz* was poor consolation to Beatty who felt he had Hipper at his mercy. Already outgunned, it would have taken very little longer for the close range and the heavier projectiles of the British ships to decide the issue over the Germans.

Critics, and there are many, argue that in return for two hits on the *Seydlitz* and one on the *Moltke,* (and the loss of the *Blücher*), the German gunners proved themselves far more accurate in return, hitting *Lion* 12 times. However the Germans were concentrating on *Lion* and the other British vessels were unscathed save for two hits on the *Tiger.* She was a new ship and her gunnery was not good, but by 1107 the ranges were such that the British ships, outnumbering the Germans four to three, one of which had almost half her guns out of action, had every chance of victory.

Beatty's subsequent despatch was so mutilated by the Admiralty that, when told that he deserved to be shot for his handling of his ships, he was forced, in the light of the Admiralty's interpretation of the battle, to agree!

It has also been said that Beatty overrated the effect of his ships' firing and that he mistook the German gun flashes for shell hits, and yet a civilian observer on board *Lion* at the time has recorded that there was no mistaking the difference between the firing of the enemy guns and the bursting of British shells.* If such a person can clearly distinguish between the two it seems hardly in doubt that Beatty should have done so, and this accusation can be dismissed as another unsubstantiated claim.

The *Lion* returned safely to base, as did the *Seydlitz,* but the nature of the damage to each was to ensure that the Germans, when they did venture forth again, were prepared for flash fires in the ammunition trunk, but the British were still not. The result was to be tragedy.

THE DARDENELLES (FEBRUARY–MARCH 1915)

The campaign of missed opportunities. The forcing of the narrows between the Aegean and the Black Sea held much promise as an alternative to the unmitigating slaughter of the deadlocked Western Front, but through inertia and chance came to naught. Originally it had been thought possible to penetrate it with warships alone, and indeed a study of German records reveals that had the problem been tackled more resolutely it would have succeeded.

The first naval attack took place on February 19 1915 and present in the 1st Division was the *Inflexible,* which had relieved the *Indomitable* on guard off the straits in case the *Goeben* ventured forth under her new flag. A long range bombardment was opened at 0950 upon the outer forts, but when it was clear that this was making very little impression, the ships weighed

A minor but interesting feature of the Dardenelles campaign was the use of dummy warships in an attempt to deceive the enemy appreciation of fleet dispositions. This is a merchantman, named then 'SS No 14', with mock-up superstructure resembling an early class of battle cruiser. It was popularly known as 'Tiger'. Note the characteristic counter stern and the extensive use of canvas screens to give the correct outline (IWM-Q3840).

anchor and drew in closer. Even so, the forts made little reply and it was not until 0445 that the nearer British battleships were taken under fire. *Inflexible* gave support to these vessels and eventually one of the forts was silenced. However that concluded the fighting for the day and the fleet withdrew.

The bombardment was renewed six days later and again on the following day; firing deliberately from anchored positions the ships of the Allied fleet eventually succeeded in silencing all the outer forts with little loss to themselves. The ships then moved on to tackle the inner forts, but progress lagged, despite the arrival of the brand-new *Queen Elizabeth* with her 15 inch guns. After much hesitance, another major effort was mounted on these much stronger defences on March 18.

Line 'A', including the *Queen Elizabeth, Inflexible, Agamemnon* and *Lord Nelson,* made the opening long range bombardment at 14,400 yards range. Heavy counter fire was encountered, including much from mobile howitzers which the ships found impossible to locate and destroy. Nevertheless much good practise was made by the modern battleships and at noon the older vessels of Line 'B' moved in to join the bombardment at short range. All seemed to be going well, and then the situation was reversed with a vengeance. Unknown to the attacking allied fleets, several rows of mines had been lain by the German-Turkish Navy and had remained uncharted and unswept. At 1354 the old French battleship *Bouvet* struck one of these mines. Her magazines detonated and within minutes she had gone. The bombardment continued unabated and no precautions were made as her loss had been credited to a hit by a heavy shell.

The *Inflexible* had been in the thick of the fighting and had received some superficial damage from enemy fire, her forebridge being hit and destroyed. Casualties however were few and the incident had in no way impeded her battleworthiness. But at 1611 hours she struck a mine and took on a heavy list. Heroic work managed to keep her afloat, and she was anchored off Tenedos Island, eventually returning home for repairs. In all, this valuable

HMS Inflexible *in dock at Malta, March 1915, repairing mine and gunfire damage sustained in the Dardenelles. Note the camouflage pattern, apparently light and dark grey. (IWM-SP1208).*

vessel was out of commission for six vital weeks and the near loss of such a modern vessel sealed the fate of the Naval Expedition in the Dardenelles. The same day had seen the loss of the British battleships *Irresistible* and *Ocean* and henceforth the general occupation of the peninsular was called for, with results as fruitless and costly as those it was staged to avoid.

PRELUDE TO JUTLAND (JANUARY 1915–MAY 1916)

The scene of major naval activity now switched back to the North Sea. Here both the Grand Fleet and the Battle Cruiser Squadron had at last found secure resting places after a miserable winter roaming around the Scottish coast, because a main base for them had not been prepared before the war.

Up to the end of January the battle cruisers had sunk three armoured cruisers and two light cruisers without loss to themselves and had been in the forefront of every major naval action. The First Lord of the Admiralty therefore came to the conclusion that this 'fast spearhead' warranted more worthy status than the title 'Battle Cruiser Squadron' implied, and accordingly he carried through the formation of the 'Battle Cruiser Fleet.' As Churchill himself was later to record.

'The central conception of this force was speed. It presented a combination of speed and power far superior to any naval force at the disposal of the Germans'.

Beatty was given control of this impressive force with the title of Fleet Commander and the ten battle cruisers were organised into three squadrons, each one under command of a Rear Admiral. To keep this force at maximum strength the *Australia,* still in the Pacific, was asked for and duly sent. In support were the new fast cruisers of the 'Arethusa' and 'Caroline' classes and the magnificent 'M' class destroyers of the 13th Flotilla then entering service, some of which were capable of almost 40 knots.

Despite the fact that it was carefully laid down that the Battle Cruiser Fleet was to remain an integral part of the Grand Fleet, the C-in-C apparently disapproved of its elevation, for on his subsequent appointment to the post of First Sea Lord in late 1916 he changed the title to the less impressive one of 'Battle Cruiser Force'!

On December 22, 1914, the *Lion* had led her sisters to anchor above the Forth Railway Bridge in the Firth of Forth, opposite the ruins of Rosyth Castle. Here, for the first time since the war began, the ships found a secure resting place between their interminable sorties into the empty North Sea. Fisher had reservations about this choice, and he had visions of the Germans bombing the bridge on the eve of a major sortie and trapping Beatty's force, but it was a great improvement over the previous bases of the force. Prior to this time they had used Invergordon and Scapa Flow, but in the Forth the battle cruisers were eight hours steaming closer to the enemy and also close to the amenities of Edinburgh, communications with the Admiralty in London also being much improved.

Opposite the anchorage, at Queensferry, the destroyer flotillas found secure berths at Port Edgar where oiling facilities were provided for them, while Rosyth dockyard was naturally fully equipped to deal with both routine maintenance and battle damage. A large YMCA hut was established ashore for local entertainment and Lady Beatty had her yacht, the *Sheelah,* fitted out as a hospital ship and moored close by the pier. In time the battle cruisers' anchorage became known as the 'Lions Lair'.

So they trained, patrolled and waited as the long winter of 1915-16 passed without a stir from the enemy. But in the spring a new German commander was appointed for the High Seas Fleet; von Scheer replaced Ingerhol, and with him came the promise of a new, more agressive outlook. So time passed until the momentous month of May 1916.

BATTLE OF JUTLAND (MAY 31, 1916)

Scheer's plan was merely an extension of the previous hit-and-run raids by Hipper's Battle Cruisers, and this time the target was destined to be Sunderland, but with the first abandonment of the unrestricted U-boat campaign the sortie had two distinctive features. Firstly it was hoped to draw out some of the Grand Fleet's Battleship strength in pursuit of Hipper and destroy it piecemeal before Jellicoe could arrive on the scene. Secondly, no less than 16 U-boats were stationed on Jellicoe's probable course in order to further weaken and deplete his force and make the odds more favourable in any subsequent encounter. The use of Zeppelins was another idea tried out to give forewarning of Jellicoe's approach, but in fact both submarines and airships failed lamentably in their appointed tasks.

In order to lure the British out, Hipper was told to show himself off the Norwegian coast early in the sortie, but such a stratagem was, unknown to Scheer, quite superfluous, for Admiralty Intelligence had ample warning of the deployment of the U-boat trap and the sailing of the High Seas Fleet. The British forces actually sailed the day before Scheer's ships put to sea to carry out their plan. The 3rd Battle Cruiser Squadron under Admiral Hood, which had been detached to Scapa Flow to carry out exercises earlier in the month, took their places until they returned.

Beatty had four of the newly-completed 'fast battleships' of the *Queen Elizabeth* class, mounting 15 inch guns and capable of almost 25 knots, under the command of Rear Admiral Evan-Thomas. These four, *Valiant, Malaya, Warspite* and *Barham,* sailed with the six ships of the 1st and 2nd Battle Cruiser Squadron from Rosyth on the evening of May 30 towards the planned rendezvous with the Grand Fleet Squadrons at 1400 hours the following day.

At 1415 hours the next day, Beatty, with his ships deployed in two columns with cruiser screen ahead and the 5th Battle Squadron five miles astern, came to the eastward limit of his patrol and accordingly brought his fleet about to the north for the meeting with the Grand Fleet, then some 65 miles to the north of him. Meanwhile, Hipper with his five battle cruisers was on a north-westerly course, slightly diverging with his British opponent. The Germans were still in blissful ignorance that the British were at sea in full strength, while the British, after so many false alarms, were already half resigned to the inevitability of another false start. It was here that fate, in the undistinguished shape of the Danish steamer *N. J. Ford,* took a hand. She was sighted by the picket line of cruisers from both British and German squadrons. They investigated, the cruiser *Galatea* and the German cruiser *Elbing,* sighted each other at extreme range and the Battle of Jutland commenced.

Elbing hit *Galatea* right away but not before the British cruiser had despatched her sighting report. This report mentioned of course, only light cruisers and the British light forces steered to lead the enemy to Beatty. Beatty was therefore unaware and uninformed of the presence of Hipper's five ships. He altered course with the 1st and 2nd Battle Cruiser Squadrons to intercept, but the 5th Battle Squadron missed the signal and by the time they had come around on the new course they had opened up a ten-mile gap. Strenuous steaming by the battleships managed to reduce this somewhat but a break in Beatty's force had resulted.

Hipper had received *Elbing's* signal which suggested a force of battleships was present and increased speed to locate and identify them. At a combined speed of over sixty miles an hour the 11 battle cruisers raced towards each other and at 1520 Beatty's two columns were sighted from the bridge of the *Lutzow,* leading Hipper's line. The German at once signalled their sighting to Admiral Scheer, forging up from astern and altered course to lure the British force into range of his C-in-C.

With smoke from his escorting destroyers obscuring the rangefinders of his battle cruisers, Beatty formed his ships into a single line ahead, and had to wait for the range to come down to 16,500 yards before they could engage. This threw away the advantage of the longer ranges of the British guns and was clearly to the delight of the Germans with their 11 inch and 12 inch weapons. At 1548 both sides opened fire at the same time. The Germans were able to make excellent practise against the racing British ships which were silhouetted against the sun.

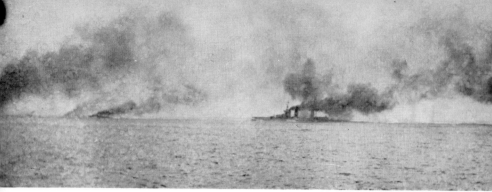

HMS Lion *being hit on 'Q' turret, Jutland, May 31, 1916. Destroyers of the 13th Flotilla are visible in the distance ahead of* Lion *(IWM-SP1704).*

Within a short time magnificent gunnery by the German ships had scored two hits on the *Lion* herself and two on the *Princess Royal,* and the *Tiger* had been hit four times. Once again there was confusion between the ships of Beatty's force, for on commencing the action he had signalled for *Princess Royal* to join *Lion* in firing at the *Lutzow,* leading Hipper's line. This meant that his other five ships were each able to engage one of Hipper's remaining vessels. But by mischance *Queen Mary* missed this signal and for a short time engaged the *Seydlitz,* the third ship in line leaving the second, the incomparable *Derfflinger,* free to make undisturbed fire at her chosen target. Luckily the *Queen Mary* soon rectified this error, and her devastating accurate salvoes were soon straddling *Derfflinger* and beginning to hit her.

Already, at 1555 she had created havoc aboard her original target *Seydlitz,* two 13·5 inch shells hitting the German vessel aft, and as at Dogger Bank, her barbette was pierced and her cordite ignited. Thanks to the lessons learned from the previous disaster her aft magazines were hastily flooded, which saved the ship. A similar situation developed aboard the *Lion* five minutes later. She had found the range and a hit was scored on the *Lutzow* but in the same instant the *Lion* was struck on 'Q' turret amidships, a weak point on all British battle cruisers.

The gun house was opened up and the cordite was set ablaze. But for the prompt action of the dying Major F. J. W. Harvey RMLI in ordering the magazine to be flooded, the flash would have gone down the trunk and torn Beatty's flagship asunder. This is what seemed to occur at the rear of the line where the *Indefatigable* had been duelling with the *Von der Tann.* The German vessel scored three devastating hits in one salvo and the *Indefatigable,* weakest ship of Beatty's force, staggered out of line mortally hit. One magazine erupted and as it did so another salvo arrived. Unable to take such mighty punishment the great ship blew up with a tremendous explosion and capsized, taking with her all save two of her 1,017 officers and men.

The pace was proving a very hot one but fortunately the 5th Battle Squadron with their mighty 15 inch guns now began to get within range and soon the *Von der Tann* and the *Moltke* received hits from them, the former vessel taking in 600 tons of water from one hit, but unlike the British ships, they did not blow up but kept in line and kept firing. *Lion* being still enveloped in smoke and flame from her earlier damage the *Seydlitz* and

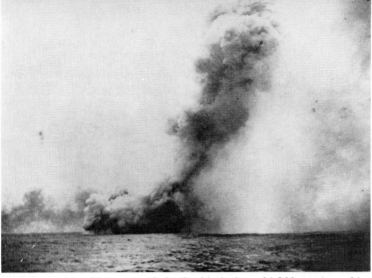

HMS Queen Mary *blows up at Jutland, with the loss of 1,266 members of her crew (IWM-SP1708).*

Derfflinger concentrated their fire on the *Queen Mary*. Ace gunnery ship of the Fleet, she had been making excellent shooting at *Seydlitz* but the British projectiles were breaking up on the German armour and not penetrating to the ships' vitals. By contrast, the inadequate protection of the British ships was proving their undoing.

The *Queen Mary* proved no more able to withstand a heavy shell concentration than had her older and weaker sister. At 1626 under the combined fire of her two opponents she was hit five times and the proud vessel split apart in an appalling explosion. Her propellers could still be seen revolving, then further explosions tore her open and she sank; 1,266 of her crew went down with her. Truly, as Beatty commented at the time, there *was* 'something wrong with our bloody ships today'.

Certainly the German battle cruisers had taken equal punishment in this stage of the encounter 'The run to the South', but they were to face further battering without loss, although all were severely damaged. Hipper was saved by the appearance of his C-in-C with the full strength of the High Seas Fleet. At 1643 Beatty, having pressed home his run to visually confirm its presence, turned his battered force to lead them towards Jellicoe, who, still unknown to Scheer, was rapidly approaching the scene of the battle.

The reverse chase, 'The run to the North', was not undertaken with vigour by the German battle cruisers, for Hipper was not so certain as his C-in-C that the Germans were chasing a beaten and detached enemy squadron. Nevertheless at 1740 Hipper's ships were again sighted by Beatty's force, now reduced to four, but with the support of Evan-Thomas's four battleships they were able to somewhat turn the tables on the enemy and a devastating fire was poured into Hipper's line. *Seydlitz* was hit and set on fire, while *Derfflinger* was badly damaged forward and began to sink by the bows. Desperate work by her damage control parties and the abandonment of the fore end of the vessel kept her afloat. Beatty had now sighted the Grand Fleet and signalled Jellicoe, 'Senior Officer Battle Cruiser Fleet to C-in-C. Have sighted enemy battle fleet bearing south-west.' He had in fact, dropped Scheer right into

The Invincible *blows up at 6.34 p.m. on May 31, 1916, Battle of Jutland.
Picture taken from* Inflexible *(IWM-SP2469).*

Jellicoe's lap. Jellicoe now made masterly deployment of the 24 huge battle-ships under his command, and the unwitting Germans suddenly found themselves steaming right into an arc of blazing guns that stretched into the distance as far as the eye could see. At this moment in the battle came another startling reminder of the inadequacies of the British battle cruisers.

Rear-Admiral Hood had led the three ships of the 3rd Battle Cruiser Squadron to the aid of Beatty, and in a superb manoeuvre brought his ships into action against the German ships ahead of the leading columns of the Grand Fleet. The *Invincible, Inflexible* and *Indomitable* began making first class shooting at the German battle cruisers. But with the range down to 10,000 yards the German ships were able to reply and the *Derfflinger* and *Lutzow* concentrated their firepower on the gallant Hood's flagship. A full salvo struck her, and again it was apparently 'Q' turret which was laid open and whose magazines exploded with the same shattering and all-consuming explosion as her two sisters earlier. Again loss of life aboard was terrible, only two officers and three ratings surviving to be picked up by her escorting destroyer *Badger.*

The loss of the three battle cruisers in similar circumstances was shattering and their sacrifice was never made good. The Germans, although in a desperate position, twice extracted themselves from the jaws of the Grand Fleet without the loss of a single heavy ship. Torpedo attacks sufficed to turn the British battleships away from their prey and in the smoke and murk of the late May afternoon Scheer evaded a massacre. During the night he penetrated the thin destroyer screen to the rear of the Grand Fleet and slipped thankfully into harbour with the loss through destroyer attack, of only one old pre-Dreadnought vessel of little fighting value.*

The German claim of a victory was obviously nonsense in view of the fact that the sole intention of the German C-in-C once he had contacted Jellicoe, was to get his ships back safely, but what should have been a devastating British victory was thrown away, with heavy losses, through caution, rigid

---

*See *Destroyer Leader,* by Peter C. Smith (Kimber, 1968) for an account of this action.

The destroyer Badger *closes on a target raft to pick up four (out of only six) survivors from* Invincible. *Bows and stern remain visible 30 minutes after the explosion. Midship portion is on sea-bed (IWM-SP2470).*

orders and the seeming lack of penetration power of British armour-piercing shells. Even the 'Death Ride of the battle cruisers', made by Hipper's already fearfully damaged ships, failed to result in the loss of a single one of them.

After Jutland, steps were taken throughout the fleet to ensure the prevention of such flash fires which were thought to have destroyed the three British heavy ships and the *Defence,* but it was too late to affect the issue. The next time the *Lion* and her sisters saw their opposite numbers was in very different circumstances.

SURRENDER OF THE HIGH SEAS FLEET (NOVEMBER 21 1918)

The supreme fulfilment of British sea power and a satisfying conclusion to the four years of patient, unrewarded waiting. The ships of the High Seas Fleet, which had mutinied after being ordered to sea in October, were met by the light cruiser *Cardiff* which led them to the rendezvous with the Grand Fleet. In full fighting trim the 224 ships of Beatty's great command, with five American and five French representative vessels, met and formed escort around the bedraggled vessels that had been the pride of the Kaiser's Germany. Included on this array of Beatty's vessels, the greatest in all Britain's naval history, were the following Battle Cruisers:

	Lion	Captain A. J. Davies
	Princess Royal	Captain J. D. Kelly
1st BCS	*Tiger*	Captain A. A. M. Duff CB
	Repulse	Captain W. H. D. Boyle CB
	Renown	Captain A. W. Craig CB
	Australia	Captain T. N. James
2nd BCS	*New Zealand*	Captain L. A. B. Donaldson CMG
	Indomitable	Captain E. K. Loring
	Inflexible	Captain J. R. P. Hawksley CB CVO
1st CS	*Courageous*	Captain A. Bromley
	Glorious	Captain C. B. Milles CB

It was the end of an epoch.

10: The 'Hood'

THE 'Mighty 'ood' was Queen of the Seas for 20 years and symbolic of everything that was best in the Royal Navy of the 'between war' period. She was perhaps one of the best loved warships of any era and certainly among the most beautiful warships to have ever graced the world's oceans. The tragedy of her origin was to mark her down over all that period of supremacy and in the final count the greatest of the British battle cruisers was to follow the *Invincible,* the first, in the same split-second annihilation.

She was the sole survivor of a class of four which had been designed in 1915 as a reply to three German 15 inch gun ships known to be under construction. In the event the German ships were stopped and with the Armistice work on three of the British giants was halted in one of the first of all too many economies.

Hood was laid down after the Battle of Jutland and was generally expected to be designed to incorporate the lessons learnt there. Side armour went up to battleship scale for the first time with a 12 inch belt at maximum, with 15 inch thick turrets and 12 inch thick barbettes. Altogether, some 5,000 tons of extra protection were added to the design after Jutland, and on her completion she had the heaviest armour yet fitted to any British warship.

As well as being the largest warship yet constructed at that time, (1920), a position she retained for almost 20 years, she presented many other distinct features which made her unique. For the first time a British capital ship dropped that useless relic, the ram bow, and she benefited from a fine clipper stem which was complemented by an almost continuous sheer combined with a strikingly flared hull.

Innovations included the adoption of the 5·5 inch gun as secondary armament, a happier choice than the triple 4 inch, but quite unsuitable 15 years later against attacks by fast aircraft. She had external bulges the whole length of her machinery and magazine spaces. Her total cost was no less than £6,025,000, (compare with *Invincible*). She reached a speed of over 32 knots on trials and was reputed to have been a steady gun platform, although always wet aft.

Magnificent she surely was, but time does not stand still, and over the

**HOOD
1941**

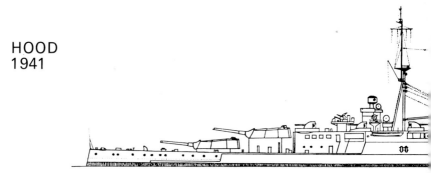

Hood   IWM—Q65664   c. 1937

long period of peace design moved on and no government was willing to pay for her to be kept in line. Finally, with war clearly imminent the money was voted for extra protection and modern anti-aircraft armament, but it was then too late. The ship that sailed to do battle with the superb *Bismarck* that spring day in 1941 was already over her permitted age limit and the tragic result of that combat was that she was blown up by a direct hit in a magazine, and sank with the loss of all but three of her crew.

Ship	Builder	Laid Down	Launched	Completed
Hood	John Brown	1.9.16	22.8.18	5.3.20

Cancelled Ships: Anson, Howe and Rodney.
Dimensions: 810' (860' OA) x 104' x $28\frac{1}{2}$'.
Displacement: 41,200 tons.
Armament: 8 x 15 inch/45; 12 x 5·5 inch/50; 4 x 4 inch AA; 6 x TT.
Machinery: Brown Curtiss turbines, 144,000 shp = 31 knots.
Complement: 1,477.

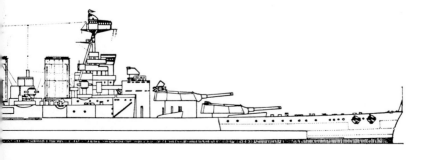

Hood

1935

IWM

11: '1921' Battle Cruisers

THIS design was the most powerful ever commenced for a British capital ship, and it is a great pity that they were not developed and used to their full potential. They embodied the most radical concepts of hull, armament and layout and would have made splendid additions to the fleet. By comparison the eventual completion of the *Nelson* and *Rodney* was a poor consolation, for they were only cut-down versions and more than ten knots slower.

Protection was to have been on a massive scale and should have even been adequate during World War 2. A 12 − 14 inch belt of armour tapered to 9 and 6 inches at its upper and lower ends. But the greatest step forward was the provision of 9 inch armour as horizontal protection over the magazines, the same as adopted by the Japanese *Yamato* 20 years later.

The secondary armament was to be mounted in twin turrets, another improvement, and anti-aircraft fire would have exceeded, on the original design, anything available in 1939 in unconverted ships. Following the Washington Conference and Treaty of 1921-22 these ships were cancelled, just one result of this event which, although called for noble purposes, resulted in a triumph for the United States, a challenge for Japan and an unprecedented disaster to Great Britain.

Henceforth the Royal Navy was reduced to the same size as that of America, a nation by no means dependent on the freedom of the seas and with at that time, no world-wide commitments. The other maritime powers actually finished proportionally stronger but the Treaty finished Great Britain as the world's greatest naval power. It also almost completes our story.

With the resumption of capital ship construction 15 years later the Battle Cruiser idea in Britain had been overtaken by events and the 'fast' battleship fulfilled the combined role for a brief period before its eventual eclipse in 1942-43 by the large, fast carrier. The German *Scharnhorst's* and the American *Guam's* were the final products of the Battle Cruiser story but are beyond the scope of this book, although they would both have delighted 'Jackie' Fisher had he lived to have seen them.

No names were officially allocated to these *1921* Class ships, although Oscar Parkes states that it was generally understood that they were to have been given the names of the first four 'I' Battle Cruisers.

Ship	Builder	Ordered	Suspended	Cancelled
1	Swan Hunter			
2	Beardmore	21.10.21	18.11.21	2.22
3	Fairfields			
4	Clydebank			

Dimensions:	820' (856' OA) x 106' x 32' 6"
Displacement:	48,000 tons.
Armament:	9 x 16 inch; 16 x 6 inch; 6 x 4·7 inch AA; 32 x 2 pdr AA; 2 x TT.
Machinery:	Geared Turbines, 160,000 shp = 32 knots
Complement:	1,716.

12: 'Renown' and 'Repulse' Modified

BOTH these vessels, in common with the *Queen Elizabeth* class battleships, underwent far-reaching modifications and re-building, the *Hood* was to have been similarly taken in hand but time ran out before the money became available. The policy adopted in the 1930s of making obsolete ships soldier on well past their safe age limit led to the inevitable losses, but has since become standard practice through no fault of the Admiralty.

'REPULSE'

In the immediate post-war period the *Repulse* was taken in hand for a major refit during which some of her deficiences in protection were rectified. Nine-inch armour replaced the 6 inch waterline belt while additional 6 inch plating was worked in along the main deck. The 4 inch guns were replaced by 3 inch HA (high angle) guns, and additional torpedo tubes were mounted.

She was still not satisfactory and as the Treaty allowed some improvements to be made to existing tonnage, a further more extensive modernisation was put in hand in 1934-36. The armament was modified to include the addition of a further pair of 4 inch guns and two pom-poms, while a hangar was added for reconnaissance aircraft together with a launching catapult. Improvements were also made to the main armament gunnery controls.

The cost of these improvements, which also included extra superstructure, amounted to some £1,300,000 but despite this she was still not really suited to front-line service when war broke out.

REPULSE
1941

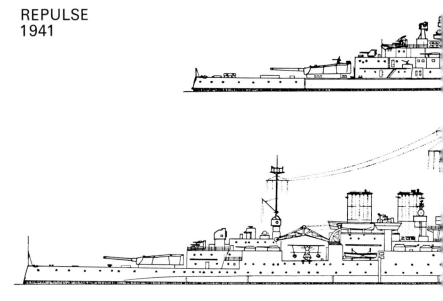

'RENOWN'

Following the precedent set by her sister, the *Renown* was refitted during 1923-26 at a cost of £979,927 which gave her similar improvements in protection and enhanced torpedo resistance with the fitting of an additional external bulge. A few pom-pom mountings were added on sponsons.

In 1936 a more far-reaching alteration was undertaken. Extra 3-4 inch armour was added over magazines and boiler rooms for protection against the type of bombing envisaged in the 1930s, and in line with this her anti-aircraft defence was very much increased by the fitting of twenty 4·5 inch DP guns disposed in four groups, each group being controlled by a separate director. Multiple pom-poms were added later, and also eight additional torpedo tubes. She was thus one of the best-prepared warships in the Royal Navy with regard to air assault when war broke out, although not enough attention had been paid to the effects of dive-bombing at sea. This oversight was to prove costly during 1940-41.

New machinery was provided in the form of Parsons geared turbines and eight Admiralty 3-drum type boilers. Developing 130,000 hp they gave the old ship 29 knots, which illustrates why the formerly lithe old lady was unable to catch the Italians at Spartivento. The former concept of the Battle Cruiser had gone by the board and the chief concern was to equip her to withstand punishment.

Extensive superstructure alterations produced a dignified matronly appearance in keeping with her age. The cost of this refit was £3,088,000 and for this money the British public got a well-balanced ship of reasonable speed at half the cost of a new vessel. The *Renown*, like the *Warspite* was to justify the cost time and time again in the years which followed.

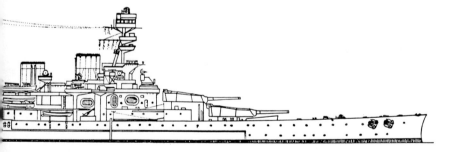

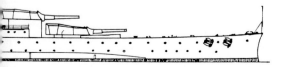

RENOWN
1939

ABOVE: HMS Repulse *leaving Portsmouth in 1936 after her modernisation refit. Compare with 1941 drawing on previous page. BELOW: Repulse in 1941. The censor has deleted the small radar aerial at the main mast-head. See drawing on previous page.*

HMS Repulse *before her 1934–36 refit showing the higher mainmast, lower midship superstructure (no hangars) and earlier fire control arrangements. There were no HA guns abreast the after superstructure and a flying-off platform remained on 'X' turret.*

13: The Passing of the Giants

THE emaciated Royal Navy which faced World War 2, which broke out on September 3 1939, contained but three Battle Cruisers, *Hood, Renown,* and *Repulse,* all of them of design dating from World War I. True, *Hood,* had a mighty reputation, and true also that *Renown* had emerged from her refit a first class vessel. The fact remained the ships were old, *Hood* badly needed modernising, which she was not to get, *Repulse* was fast but her protection, never good, was at this stage in her life completely inadequate in all respects, and on one occasion Admiral Somerville refused to have her as an addition to his sorely stretched forces on account of her lack of AA firepower.

The new German Navy was likewise much smaller, but conversely it contained in its two brand-new Battle Cruisers, *Scharnhorst* and *Gneisenau,* and its three 'Pocket' Battleships, *Admiral Graf Spee, Admiral Scheer* and

Lutzow (*Deutschland*), a total heavy ship complement whose only opponents, ie those vessels who could both hope to catch them and also match their firepower, were the three British veterans. In the event, the German ships were used with more caution than *élan* and timid High Command restrictions hampered their operations much more than was expected. There were no full scale fleet actions of capital ships against capital ships during World War 2 in the Atlantic or Mediterranean; the *Luftwaffe* controlled the North Sea up until 1942 and the British were quickly bundled out of the Pacific and so never came up against the Japanese modernised 'Kongos'. Nevertheless the three British Battle Cruisers saw considerable action and played a notable part in the final operations of the big gun warship.

DUEL OFF SKOMVAER (APRIL 9 1940)

The confused situation which prevailed at the commencement of the German invasion of Norway was enhanced by the fact that the British had begun their own limited action off the Norwegian coast at the same time. Several forces of minelaying destroyers were engaged in sowing their cargoes in the Norwegian 'Leads' and both the *Repulse* and the *Renown* were at sea to provide heavy support if needed.

For the occupation of Narvik the Germans employed ten large destroyers laden with troops, with *Scharnhorst* and *Gneisenau* out in support. The *Renown*, flying the flag of Admiral Whitworth, had lost touch with one of her four screening destroyers, the *Gloworm*, which had run into the *Hipper* and been sunk. Once the first confused reports of the German movements began to filter in, the Admiralty took precautions on the initial assumption that German heavy ships were breaking out into the Atlantic. Only later was it realised what their true mission was.

The weather on the night of April 8 was atrocious. *Renown* had rendezvoused with a force of nine destroyers off the Skomvaer Light at the southern tip of the Lofoten Islands, and stood out to sea to bar the way for the expected German break out. The ten German destroyers en route for Narvik were thus able to penetrate Vestifiord undetected. Once news of the enemy intentions was revealed Whitworth signalled his intentions to return to Vestifiord but the terrible gale which was raging necessitated that his squadron first ride out the mountainous seas which made the destroyers' operations nigh impossible. The C-in-C Home Fleet meantime despatched *Repulse* and the cruiser *Penelope* to reinforce him.

Meanwhile, in the same raging seas the *Scharnhorst* and the *Gneisenau* had turned north-west to carry out a diversionary mission in the Arctic while the troops got ashore in Norway. Some 50 miles west of Skomvaer at 0337 on the morning of April 9 the *Renown* caught a brief glimpse of a heavy warship which she identified as *Gneisenau*. In the murk and blackness the second Battle Cruiser was taken for a *Hipper* class cruiser. *Renown* worked up to 20 knots through the towering seas, at which speed the destroyers could not keep in touch, and quickly closed on the unsuspecting German vessels. With the range down to 19,000 yards *Renown* opened the action against the two most powerful units of the German Navy at 0405.

The German Admiral Lütjens was first aware of the presence of British heavy ships when *Renown's* opening salvo arrived. Some six minutes elapsed before *Gneisenau* was able to answer, but on a parallel course the two German ships were able to reply to *Renown's* six 15 inch guns with 18 11 inch guns. Despite the conditions in which the battle was fought the big

Renown *(in action at Spartivento)* IWM–A6412 1940

ships soon began to register on each other and *Renown* took two heavy shells which failed to penetrate and in return she punished Lütjens' flagship severely. One of her one-ton projectiles struck the foretop of the *Gneisenau* and destroyed her main fire control system, this rendered her main batteries useless until control was switched to an auxiliary position. Although far out of the picture some of the little British destroyers had tried their luck with their 4·7 inch guns and the flashes of these seemed to convince Lütjens that he had too much to handle. He brought *Gneisenau* round on a north-easterly course while the *Scharnhorst* made smoke.

The action now developed into a chase with the ancient *Renown* pursuing the two German ships right into the teeth of a raging gale. Twice more her gunners scored on the German flagship, the first pierced the range-finder hood on *Gneisenau's* fore turret which in the stormy conditions soon flooded, while the second demolished one of her anti-aircraft gun positions. At 28 knots the German ships plunged into the murk and Whitworth eased down and drew away to the NE to avoid the worst of the weather.

After a short interval the Germans were again sighted and it was seen that they had increased the range. The duel opened again, the *Renown* working up to 29 knots but still being unable to close. The enemy eventually ran clear and *Renown* came about to ensure that they did not work their way around to the south of her. In fact the Germans seemed to have only one intention and that was to escape from the old veteran who had given them such a fight. The high-speed steaming into the face of the storm resulted in each of the German Battle Cruisers having a turret put out of action.

Thus ended the only battle between rival Battle Cruisers in World War 2. Inconclusive and brief, it nevertheless set the pattern for all other surface actions the Royal Navy undertook in that conflict. There was absolutely no hesitancy about Whitworth's actions.

BATTLE OF SPARTIVENTO (NOVEMBER 27 1940)

With the entry of Italy into the war and the collapse of France, the control of the Mediterranean was in some doubt. The Italian fleet comprised four old, but modernised battleships, with two brand-new ships just being completed, and two more under construction. The main Mediterranean Fleet under the command of Admiral Cunningham lay at Alexandria, four old battleships and a carrier. To hold the sea routes from the west Admiral Sir James Somerville was appointed to the command of Force 'H', built around the *Renown,* the *Ark Royal,* the cruiser *Sheffield* and six destroyers of the 8th flotilla. Various additional ships were added to this force when available. Its principal task developed into providing the heavy cover for convoys running through to Malta.

The main units of Force H at sea, HMS Renown, *leading* Ark Royal *and* Sheffield. *The disposition of the 4·5 inch high angle batteries in* Renown *can be clearly seen (IWM).*

Towards the end of November 1940 a series of operations took place which were in the main unopposed by the Italians save for moderate air attacks. However, their main fleet was still a factor to be reckoned with, even after the battles of Calabria and Taranto. Operation *Collar* was set in train from Gibraltar on November 25. Three freighters made up the convoy, two light transports, *Manchester* and *Southampton* were carrying RAF and military personnel to Malta, and four corvettes were to join Cunningham's fleet. To escort these Somerville had ships of Force 'H' as described above with the addition of the cruiser *Despatch* and the destroyers *Kelvin, Jaguar, Wishart, Hotspur* and *Encounter* as close escort. He was also to rendezvous with the old battleship *Ramillies*, cruisers *Newcastle, Coventry* and *Berwick* west of Malta to effect the change over of escorts and bring *Ramillies* back.

The operation proceeded without incident until the morning of November 27 when, at 0852 one of *Ark Royal's* Swordfish aircraft sighted a group of warships and reported four cruisers and six destroyers. Unfortunately this sighting report was not picked up by the ships. Not until 0956 was a signal confirmed and passed to Somerville, who at once deployed his forces in the anticipation that this might be the enemy and not *Ramillies'* force.

At 1016 further spotter reports confirmed the presence of battleships among the force, now clearly Italian, and Force 'H' altered course to engage. The three 'Town' class cruisers were stationed in the van with the destroyers stationed at 050 degrees five miles from *Renown* on the estimated bearing of the enemy, and speed was increased to 28 knots.

The Italian force actually consisted of two battleships, seven cruisers and sixteen destroyers under Admiral Campioni. Hopes were now high in Force 'H' of imminent action and at 1128 *Ramillies, Berwick, Newcastle* and destroyers joined with Somerville's force, but *Ramillies* was unable to stand the pace of what soon became another headlong chase. The Italians feared that they were facing a superior force, the air strikes by *Ark Royal's* Swordfish torpedo bombers, although inflicting no damage, worried them and they turned for home.

At 1207 the *Renown* reported an overheating bearing which reduced her speed to $27\frac{1}{2}$ knots but almost at once the enemy cruisers were sighted on the horizon and the engagement opened at extreme ranges. The Italians opened fire at 1220, to which the British in the van replied, *Renown* commenced firing at 1224. Here targets were the 8 inch armed enemy cruisers, which she engaged at 26,500 yards with six salvoes. The Italians laid smoke and continued on their course. *Ramillies* never got into range as her best speed was only 20 knots and she soon fell astern.

Renown altered course to clear the arcs of all guns and recommenced firing with salvoes at another cruiser target. Eight salvoes were fired and then this target too was obscured by smoke. The Italian return salvoes were accurate and *Berwick* was hit, although she stayed in the fight. The enemy continued to withdraw at high speed and further attacks by the Fleet Air Arm failed to stop them. One heavy cruiser was reported as hit by a heavy shell and on fire aft. Fire was checked for a time through lack of targets, and the at 1311 *Renown* came into action again against further Italian heavy cruisers, but at extreme distance.

By 1330 the enemy were well under the shelter of their shore-based bomber squadrons and in view of the fact that they were still pulling away at superior speed Admiral Somerville decided to abandon the chase and return to cover his convoy. Again the results were disappointing to the *Renown's* crew but their morale was further enhanced to know that both the newest German ships and the brand new *Vittorio Veneto* adopted the same policy when confronted with their ship. As Admiral Somerville subsequently wrote:

'It was a pleasure to observe the enthusiasm with which the ship's company of *Renown* closed up at their action stations on hearing that enemy forces were in the vicinity and their subsequent disappointment when it was clear that the enemy did not intend to stand and fight was obvious.'*

Thus ended *Renown's* fleeting contacts with the second Axis partner.

Somerville's Despatch (London Gazette, May 1948).

THE 'BISMARCK' EPISODE (MAY 21—28 1941)

After she had completed her working-up trials the new German battleship *Bismarck,* (42,500 tons, 8 x 15 inch guns), sailed for Norway. It had originally been the intention for her to go with her sister ship, *Tirpitz,* out into the Atlantic and fall upon the British convoy routes. Such a powerful combination as these two vessels would have presented the Admiralty with their gravest threat yet. As it was the *Tirpitz* was not ready and so *Bismarck's* companion was the new heavy cruiser, *Prinz Eugen,* (14,500 tons, 8 x 8 inch). Even this duo poised so serious a threat that the whole of the heavy ship complement of the Royal Navy available for North Atlantic duty was called upon to bring them to bay.

All three Battle Cruisers were theoretically available, although the *Renown,* with Force 'H' at Gibraltar, was not expected to play any role. With the C-in-C Home Fleet was the *Hood,* which, together with the newly-completed and not yet fully worked-up battleship, *Prince of Wales,* was sent out under the command of Vice-Admiral L. E. Holland to guard the Denmark Strait and the Faroes-Iceland passage. The *Repulse* was at the Clyde with the aircraft carrier *Victorious,* ready to escort a convoy to Gibraltar. She and the carrier subsequently joined the C-in-C whose flag was in *King George V.* This force sailed to cover the area south of *Hood's* squadron should the German squadron evade them.

Bismarck herself sailed on the sortie but was detected in the Denmark Strait on May 23 by the cruiser *Suffolk,* which with her sister ship the *Norfolk* held the German squadron until Vice-Admiral Holland's force arrived on the scene at 0530 on the morning of the next day. The German ships' fates now appeared sealed. *Hood* was rated the best gunnery vessel in the fleet, and with the *Prince of Wales* in support as well as two heavy cruisers the single German battleship and one heavy cruiser were completely outgunned. Unfortunately Holland's six destroyers had been detached before the engagement and their invaluable support with torpedo attack was therefore thrown away. Even so the contest was to the British advantage and with the whole day in which to do battle there was thought to be no chance of the Germans slipping away.

Aboard the *Hood* instant readiness for action was ordered at 0510 and the German squadron was sighted at 0535 on the starboard beam and a long way off. Holland at once turned his two ships 40 degrees towards the enemy to close the range quickly and at 0549 he turned his squadron another 20 degrees in towards the enemy. Such an acute angle of approach masked the arcs of the British vessels' after turrets. With both the British ships' 'A' arcs closed the action commenced.

Because the silhouettes of the two German vessels were very similar the action opened with the *Hood* firing at the *Prinz Eugen* and the *Prince of Wales* taking on the *Bismarck.* With a mistake reminding one of the Dogger Bank battle the German flagship was thus left reasonably undisturbed to concentrate her full broadside armament on the *Hood.*

Hood opened fire at 0552 with the range at 25,000 yards and *Bismarck* replied almost at once. *Prince of Wales* commenced firing at the same time as did *Prinz Eugen.* *Hood's* first salvoes were noted by observers to be very accurate, and the third was a straddle. *Prince of Wales* with a faulty gun in 'A' turret took longer to find the range but was straddling the target by her sixth salvo. The Germans were as always, superbly accurate right from the start and the cruiser with her more rapid rate of fire scored a hit on the

Hood in under a minute. A large fire broke out close by the mainmast which burnt fiercely for a while and then glowed and pulsated. In return the *Bismarck* was hit by a 14 inch shell from *Prince of Wales.*

The range was now to Holland's satisfaction and at 0555 he signalled for a 20 degree turn to port in order to allow the British ships to fire full broadsides. As the turn commenced the *Bismarck,* which had already straddled the *Hood* and perhaps already hit her once, dealt the British vessel her death blow.

Onlookers saw two towering splashes close alongside the Battle Cruiser and then there was a vast eruption of flame from between her masts as *Bismarck's* fifth salvo penetrated her vitals at a range of 16,500 yards. A sheet of flame blossomed into the sky a thousand feet, her back broken in the colossal explosion; briefly through the smoke her bows and stern could be seen rising. In two minutes she had gone and the *Prince of Wales* had to make a sharp alteration of course to avoid ploughing through the area of her flagship's destruction.

The *Bismarck* now switched targets and the *Prince of Wales* quickly received hits from her 15 inch shells which smashed into her bridge, killing almost every man there, and also destroyed her secondary armament control and spotter aircraft installation. This coupled with further defects in her main turrets necessitated her breaking off the action, for *Bismarck* appeared unaffected. The Germans made no attempt to pursue her, had they done so it is possible that she would have joined *Hood* on the bottom.

The tragic *Hood,* destroyed in her first action after only a few minutes firing, went down at 63° 20'N, 31° 50'W, some 500 miles north-east of Cape Farewell, with her went the reputation of the Royal Navy's Battle Cruisers. As Ernle Bradford was to record in *The Mighty Hood* (Hodder):

> 'The greatest and most graceful ship of her time, perhaps of any time, she was the last of the Leviathans—those mighty ships, whose movements on the high seas had determined policy since the last quarter of the nineteenth century. A generation of British seamen had been trained in her. To millions of people she had represented British seapower and imperial might. With her passed not only a ship, but a whole era, swept away on the winds of the world'.

There were only three survivors from her crew, and 94 officers and 1,321 men went to their deaths.

The subsequent chase and final despatch of the *Bismarck* ensured the revenge of the *Hood.* The *Repulse* would have been far too weak a vessel to join in combat with the German ship if brought to bay without massive support but as it was she ran short of fuel during the search and had to be sent into Newfoundland. Her place was taken by the terribly slow but stronger *Rodney* more able to stand up for herself. The *Renown* too was denied the chance of engaging the *Bismarck* and avenging her sister although Admiral Somerville was dubious of even her chances in a straight fight, as well he might have been.

The crew of the *Renown* felt quite confident and were convinced that their ship was kept out of the last actions which destroyed the German Battleship to enable other, 'unblooded' vessels to have a chance!

DISASTER OFF KUANTAN (DECEMBER 10 1941)

It had long been the intention of the Admiralty to despatch strong naval forces to Singapore should the threat of Japanese invasion materialise, but when the shattering blow of Pearl Harbour took place on December 7 the Navy found itself hard pressed in every theatre and in the event all that could be found to provide the nucleus of a main fleet were the *Prince of Wales* and the *Repulse* and four destroyers. Several other vessels, the heavy cruiser *Exeter,* Australian units and a few ancient destroyers, were to join them, as was the new carrier *Indomitable,* but events overtook these plans.

The Japanese had already been in occupation of French Indo-China and had based there several crack squadrons of land-based naval bomber squadrons containing both high level and torpedo-bomber elements. In their invasion plans they had also two battleships in a covering force for their troop transports, but these were not finally needed.

The two British heavy ships had arrived at Singapore on December 2 but if sent as a deterrent they arrived too late and were not powerful enough to affect the issue, for Japan was fully prepared. The first actual reports of landings were received by the British at dawn on December 8 but reports of the Japanese troop convoys steaming west had been received as early as two days before that. Without air cover Admiral Philips had a delicate problem on his hands, but he finally decided to sortie out against these convoys and destroy them rather than 'hide among the innumerable islands', as Churchill suggested. The latter policy would do nothing to deter the enemy and would merely lower the morale of his own men, it was not to *avoid* the enemy that the two big ships had been sent to Malayan waters.

Accordingly Philips took his squadron to sea on the evening of December 8 and sortied north to find the enemy transports believed to be disgorging their troops at either Kota Bharu or Singora. Unfortunately the British force was soon sighted by a Japanese submarine and the 22nd Naval Air Flotilla, which had been bombed up ready for an attack on Singapore from Saigon airfields, was hastily re-armed with torpedoes and sent on a search for Philip's squadron.

All the RAF's fighters had been withdrawn to Singapore island to deal with expected air raids, and Philips had been informed on sailing that no fighter cover would be available at dawn on December 10, nevertheless he pressed on, not knowing he had been sighted by the enemy, in the hope of making a sudden surprise appearance among the enemy transports, sinking them, and withdrawing out of range before the Japanese could retaliate. However the aircraft of the Japanese Navy were in no way to be compared with the obsolete Swordfish and Fulmars with which the Royal Navy's Air Arm was equipped at this time, and the modern bombers of the 22nd Flotilla had adequate range to cover Philips' withdrawal routes.

While at sea a report was received of enemy landings at Kuantan, half-way down the eastern Malayan coast and Philips therefore sent the destroyer *Express* in to check this. It turned out to be a false alarm but the delay proved conclusive. The Japanese had despatched nine scout planes to find the British squadron at dawn on December 10 and these were followed into the air by no less than 34 high-level bombers and 50 torpedo-bombers.

They had missed the British ships on their outward flight but on their return leg they picked them up. Soon after 1100 the first formation was seen from the bridge of *Repulse.*

Eleven bombers were in this wave and they concentrated their attack on the old Battle Cruiser, which Admiral Somerville had feared could not face up to prolonged air assault. The anti-aircraft barrage thrown up by the two capital ships was not heavy nor was it accurate. There had been little opportunity to practise and the *Prince of Wales* had only had some of her Bofors guns bolted into position the day before the sortie, in Singapore dockyard! The Japanese held their formation and they bombed remarkably accurately, hitting *Repulse* with one bomb on the armoured deck beneath the hangar, but it failed to penetrate.

Some 20 minutes later a torpedo-bomber attack developed against both ships. The Japanese dropped their torpedoes from a height of 300 feet, much to the British crews' surprise, as common practice was for torpedo-bombers to come down to some 20 or 30 feet. Captain Tennant kept his course steady until the aircraft actually dropped and then manoeuvred *Repulse* to comb the tracks. She thus escaped unscathed but the *Prince of Wales* was not so fortunate and she took two hits which reduced her speed to 20 knots and gave her an 11 degree list which incapacitated half her AA armament.

At 1155 another high-level attack was directed against *Repulse* but this time she managed to avoid being hit although the Japanese bombed very accurately again. Tennant now closed with his flagship, which was not under control, to render aid, and as he did so another determined torpedo-bomber assault developed. This attack was very skilfully made in two waves and the *Repulse* was hit abreast the after funnel by one torpedo, but she absorbed it well and was still capable of 25 knots. *Prince of Wales*, unable to manoeuvre, took three or four hits.

The Japanese attack now grew to a climax and several waves deployed at once. There was no avoiding the many torpedoes dropped in this assault and the old *Repulse* was struck by four more on both sides. Within a few minutes she had listed over, her rudders jammed. Captain Tennant recognised that she was finished and ordered the crew to abandon ship. As they took to the water the *Repulse* rolled right over and went down. Crippled and in extreme difficulties the *Prince of Wales* fell easy prey to another high-level attack but only one bomb struck her and this failed to penetrate her armour. Once again, as occurred over and over again throughout the war, high-level bombing proved useless. But the damage caused by the torpedoes was enough without this and at 0120 the *Prince of Wales* capsized, taking with her Admiral Philips and her Captain, and 500 men. As she went down the first RAF fighters arrived overhead.

THE LAST DAYS (1942–45)

With the *Hood* and *Repulse* gone only the *Renown* remained of Britain's Battle Cruisers. She was to stay the fastest capital ship in the Royal Navy for the rest of the war. Her subsequent life was not without action as her war record shows. She was present when the Royal Navy again started to assert itself in the Indian Ocean and struck back for the *Repulse* in the bombardment of Sabang in 1943. But with the end of the war, this grand old ship, now over 30 years old, was obviously unsuited to the needs of the post-war fleet, and in 1948, in company with many equally famous veterans, like *Nelson, Rodney* and *Royal Sovereign,* she went to the breakers. It was, as one Lord of the Admiralty stated at the time, like saying farewell to some very old friends. Not a single British capital ship has been preserved to remind the nation of the 300 years during which Britain remained secure behind the shield provided by the big-gun warship in all its many forms.

Of those 300 or more years the Battle Cruiser held pride of place for a mere ten, then Jutland showed up their weakness. For a further 30 the ships of the type, in progressively fewer numbers, continued to serve, and took, in proportion to their numbers, as large a part in World War 2 as in the First. Misconceived and tragic ships as they were, their beauty, grace and power overrode their faults and hid their failings.

APPENDIX ONE
Table to compare the growth of the Type

Class	Tonnage	Armament	Speed
Invincible	17,250	8 x 12 in.	25 knots.
Indefatigable	18,800	8 x 12 in.	25 knots.
Lion	26,350	8 x 13·5 in.	27 knots.
Tiger	28,500	8 x 13·5 in.	28 knots.
Renown	27,500	6 x 15 in.	30 knots.
Courageous	18,600	4 x 15 in.	31 knots.
Hood	41,200	8 x 15 in.	31 knots.
1921 Class	48,000	9 x 16 in.	32 knots.

APPENDIX TWO
The German Ships

Class	Tonnage	Armament	Speed
Von der Tann	19,100	8 x 11 in. 10 x 5·9 in.	26 knots.
Moltke	22,640	10 x 11 in. 12 x 5·9 in.	27 knots.
Seydlitz	24,610	10 x 11 in. 12 x 5·9 in.	27 knots.
Derfflinger	26,180	8 x 12 in. 14 x 5·9 in.	27 knots.
Scharnhorst	31,500	9 x 11 in. 12 x 5·9 in.	32 knots.

APPENDIX THREE
BATTLE CRUISER PENDANTS
(No flag superior)

Ship	Oct 1914	Jan 1918	March 1918
Inflexible	83	75	47
Indomitable	77	74	05
Invincible	85	—	—
Australia	C6	09	81
Indefatigable	13	—	—
New Zealand	08	90	53
Lion	22	79	67
Princess Royal	29	95	68
Queen Mary	14	—	—
Tiger	42	A4	91
Courageous	—	51	94
Glorious	—	67	56
Repulse	54	0A	26
Renown	64	99	23

	1939–45
Hood	51
Renown	72
Repulse	34